# *the Quality Auditor's Handbook*

# *the Quality Auditor's Handbook*

Don L. Freeman

To join a Prentice Hall Internet mailing list,
point to http://www.prenhall.com/mail_lists.

Prentice Hall PTR, Upper Saddle River, New Jersey 07458

Library of Congress Cataloging-in-Publication Data

Editorial/Production Supervision: *Joe Czerwinski*
Acquisitions Editor: *Bernard Goodwin*
Editorial Assistant: *Diane Spina*
Manufacturing Manager: *Alexis R. Heydt*
Cover Design Director: *Jerry Votta*
Cover Design: *Design Source*
Marketing Manager: *Miles Williams*

© 1997 by Prentice Hall PTR
Prentice-Hall, Inc.
A Division of Simon and Schuster
Upper Saddle River, NJ 07458

Prentice Hall books are widely used by corporations and government agencies for training, marketing, and resale. The publisher offers discounts on this book when ordered in bulk quantities. For more information, contact:

Corporate Sales Department
Phone: 800-382-3419
Fax: 201-236-7141
E-mail: corpsales@prenhall.com

Or write

Prentice Hall PTR
Corp. Sales Dept.
One Lake Street
Upper Saddle River, NJ 07458

All rights reserved. No part of this book may be reproduced in any form or by any means, without permission in writing from the publisher.

Printed in the United States of America

10 9 8 7 6 5 4 3 2 1

ISBN: 0-13-268202-8

Prentice-Hall International (UK) Limited, London
Prentice-Hall of Australia Pty. Limited, Sydney
Prentice-Hall of Canada Inc., Toronto
Prentice-Hall Hispanoamericana, S.A., Mexico
Prentice-Hall of India Pte. Ltd., New Delhi
Prentice-Hall of Japan, Inc., Tokyo
Simon & Schuster Asia Pte. Ltd., Singapore
Editora Prentice-Hall do Brasil, Ltda., Rio de Janeiro

# CONTENTS

# PREFACE

Auditing is so many things all wrapped into one activity that is very difficult to find that perfect analogy to describe it. Auditing is detective work and it is a quest. It is often an adventure on which hidden things that might have never come to light without an auditor's persistence and determination are discovered and brought into the bright light of day. It is also a simple human activity. We can define auditing. We can categorize audits. We can try to expand the definition to include all sorts of other purposes—and end up confusing the issue—but, in the end, we still have a hard time coming up with that one analogy that pins auditing down like a butterfly in cotton.

One thing is sure. The more we work with auditing, the more we come to value the idea and the purpose of auditing. At best, we might have had this notion that audits were some kind of necessary evil. They were a silly activity carried out by nit-pickers who came around to make sure that all the I's were dotted and the T's were crossed, but who added no value to our products, processes, or business. More often than not, we viewed the audit as a nuisance, sometimes even as a detriment to our success. There has been some truth to this. Auditing has been overused in some industries. It has become a drag on the success of companies within these industries, an unnecessary and heavy burden for some companies to carry. At other times and in other industries, auditing has become nothing more than a perfunctory exercise. The auditors go through the same steps time after time. Both the auditor and the person being audited know what the steps are—and they go through them all with the bored familiarity of an airline ticket agent asking if you packed your own bags. So with this kind of background, when we come to examine auditing our first reaction might be, "Do I have to?" However, if we come to auditing with a new, fresh approach, or maybe with a reaffirmation of some forgotten fundamental values, it isn't long before we begin to develop an appreciation for auditing, for what auditing can—and *should*—be.

I can include a note about my personal journey and discovery here. Some years ago, when I got started in the ISO 9000 business, I approached the whole idea of auditing as I might clearing roadkill off the road: something stinky and festering that had to be done. After all, the ISO standard required it. We had to do it. We might not like it, but we had to do it. I knew enough to know that I would never get it done if I taught auditing in that fashion, so I had to come up with some enthusiasm for the game. I did. I jumped into auditing with renewed zeal. I specialized in internal audits, and over the years trained hundreds of internal auditors and put dozens of internal audit programs in place. And my conversion didn't take long. Without exception, internal audit programs became valuable to the company. What was once viewed as roadkill became an integral part of the company's success. I became a convert, something of a zealot. Forgive me, but I have empirical evidence—*objective evidence*—for my enthusiasm.

From a nuisance activity, from a detrimental activity, auditing has become a value-added activity.

Most of us have had some experience with audits and auditors, directly or indirectly. Those with financial backgrounds have participated in financial audits. Those with safety, environmental, or nuclear energy backgrounds are also familiar with audits and auditors. Maybe your experience has been limited to being audited—being in the "hot seat." Well, that taught you something about audits and auditors—even if it is nothing more than to avoid them at all costs.

And here you are reading a book about auditing, perhaps taking the first step on the path to becoming an auditor yourself.

You have seen the enemy, and it is you!

Most people who pick up this book, whether as an individual or as part of an organized class, are neophyte auditors. A good number of them are not even sure they want to be auditors. Most are nervous about the prospect. Some are even looking for the exit signs right now and moving over that way so they can get out of here fast.

Relax. I know it's a lot easier to say than to do, but really, there's nothing to worry about. Step right up and try on the auditor's shoes. There is nothing to fear. There's even a good possibility you might like being an auditor.

## What's in This Book—and How Will It Help You?

If you are new to the auditing game, or if you need a little refresher, this is the book for you. It is different from other books about auditing on the shelves because it is as close to "how to" as I can get it. This is not a book about theory. It is a book about how to audit. This is a book to help the auditor in all phases of auditing. There is some discussion about theory, principles, and concepts of auditing. But this is only so we can all start on the same sheet of music. There is also a discussion of how the ISO 9000 international standard has influenced quality system auditing, and how it may be used as a guideline for auditors.

The bulk of the book is aimed at helping the auditor to plan, conduct, and report the results of an audit. It begins with how audits are planned and provides the auditor with serviceable tools. Then it talks about how an audit is conducted, giving sound, practical hints about techniques to make audits most effective. It concludes with how to document the findings of an audit.

The approach this book takes is sequential and logical. Read it and it will give the prospective auditor insight into process and principles, but the auditor needn't stop there. The book is a true guideline and a valuable reference tool. Auditors will come back to this book time and time again over their career as auditors.

## Some Notes About Why This Book Was Written

My idea when I started developing this book was to provide neophyte auditors with as many practical, "nuts-and-bolts" guidelines about auditing as I could. I saw a need for such a thing, because the widespread application of ISO 9001/2 requires an ongoing internal audit program. I was training auditors all over the country in companies applying ISO, and the most common habit was for the company to appoint people to be trained as auditors. These people, more often than not, had no auditing experience. They understood the value and the importance of the program, but they came to the game with very little knowledge about how it is played.

Some training organizations' approach was to steep these folks in the theory of auditing. As I said, these people understood the value and importance of auditing. What they needed was some practical help to hit the ground running.

I had an opportunity to develop the internal auditor training for the headquarters of a large corporation. The training manager of this corporation didn't know anything about ISO or auditing, but he knew a lot about training. He was concerned that the training be practical and performance-based, with measurable results. So was I. A two-day time frame was agreed upon, with an additional day of practice audits. Two days doesn't allow a lot of playing around. And it was our desire to incorporate many exercises in the program.

Rather than rely upon lecture to drive across some of the important concepts about auditing, I chose to build an extensive handbook and lecture only on the high points of the handbook. This approach depended upon the participants to review concepts in the handbook on their own. It turned out to be very successful—judging from the performance of the auditors in practice—in spite of the reading level of most Americans.

Over the years, the handbook grew. I built my own version of that training and I have exported it all over the United States and even to Mexico. I have tried to incorporate tidbits and hints as I came across them into the handbook, and the handbook has grown into the book you now hold in your hands.

Let me repeat the goal of this book: to provide a practical guide to the neophyte auditor. You won't find a lot of auditing theory in this book. For the new auditor, it will, I hope, become a tool kit and valuable resource. For the manager of audit programs, it will provide a basis for training novice auditors.

I rely heavily upon ISO 9000 in this book. It is what I have been working with for some years. It would be a mistake, however, to think of this handbook as merely an ISO 9000 auditing handbook. The practices and tools discussed and shown in this book can be modified and used with any other type of quality system auditing, no matter what the foundation, indeed, they could be used for other types of auditing as well, such as environmental auditing (ISO14000).

A note about the style of this book. I have tried to keep it as bright and as breezy as I can without sacrificing the importance of the activity. My desire was to make it eminently readable.

For this handbook to meet its stated goal it needs to be open to new ideas and methods. I would like to extend an invitation to the readers of this book to contribute their ideas. I will endeavor to incorporate them in new editions of this handbook.

Lastly, there are a number of people who directly or indirectly helped me with this handbook. All my British friends who dragged me (almost kicking and screaming) into auditing—Derrick, Carolyn, John, David, and Dennis. They all contributed. Mark, the training manager, didn't know I was aiming for a book, but he provided the right framework to make my idea a reality. And there are two auditors out there with whom I have worked over the years whose brains I have picked over so much I'm surprised they have anything left: David and Bert. I suppose, in a way, the biggest thanks should go out to all the hundreds of students I have had. They always brought energy and enthusiasm and they always pointed me in new directions.

If I have left anyone out, forgive me. It was done in forgetfulness and not out of malice.

# *the Quality Auditor's Handbook*

CHAPTER 1

# What Is Quality Auditing?

## Introduction

The place to begin in achieving an understanding of what quality auditing is at the beginning. Let's go back to the basic foundation and get a working definition of quality auditing. Just what are we talking about?

There are a lot of definitions of what quality auditing is. Though there are many, they also share many aspects in common. My personal selection for a good working definition of a quality audit comes from an ISO (International Standards Organization) publication, ISO 8402, *Quality Vocabulary.*

**A quality audit is:**

"A systematic and independent examination to determine if quality activities and related results comply with planned arrangements and whether these arrangements have been implement effectively and are suitable to achieve objectives."

This is a pretty good working definition. There are similar definitions published by other organizations and they all share certain aspects in common.

Sometimes the word investigation is used in place of *examination*. Personally, I favor examination, because it is less threatening than investigation. Whether investigation or examination, the activity remains the same: the auditor is looking into something—examining (investigating) something.

- It is a *systematic* examination, which simply means it is carried out in a methodical, systematic manner. It isn't done from the hip or willy-nilly. Auditing is a planned activity, approached and carried out in a systematic manner, and it is part of a larger system.
- Auditing is an *independent* examination. The requirement for independence is one of the key factors in successful quality auditing. What does independence mean? The best explanation comes from the words of ISO 9001/2, paragraph 4.17, which states, "...shall be carried out by personnel having no direct responsibility for the areas being audited." This directly translates into "you can't audit your own work!" Just as a passing note, a lot of organizations use the term self-audit for review activities carried on within a department or an activity. While this may be a good practice, it shouldn't be called a self-audit. With this definition, there can be no such thing.
- This systematic and independent examination is conducted *"...to determine if quality activities and related results comply with planned arrangements..."*. Now we are getting to the heart of quality auditing. Why do we conduct quality audits? It is to find out if an organization is doing what it said it was going to do. This sets up in our minds as we read it, one of the principal activities going on during an audit: a comparison of one thing against another.

- Another reason for this systematic and independent examination is to determine if *"...these arrangements are implemented effectively...."* This is a little redundant. If an organization is not doing what is said it was going to do, then its system has not been implemented.
- The information captured by this systematic and independent examination will help determine if the arrangements are *"...suitable to achieve objectives."* This phrase does a couple of very interesting things. It injects a value judgment into the auditing process and it also broadens the scope of the audit. If you read the definition carefully up to this point, you find there is no room for value judgments, no subjectivity. Now this changes. And this sets up a problem. Auditors, by and large, don't make value judgments. The auditor examines and records results but does not make any value judgments. Also, the auditor rarely sees an entire system. The auditor, generally, only sees a part, or parts, of the system. But this phrase gives us insight into the higher purpose of audits. The auditor gathers information, and someone uses this information to determine policy or process. Someone uses the auditor's information to make value judgments about the effectiveness of the system. Is it suitable to achieve objectives? Is it helping us do what we set out to do? That someone is management. Management uses the information gathered and recorded by auditors.

Now with this definition we have a common starting place. We are all starting together, singing from the same sheet of music, as the old saying goes. Now that we have an idea of what we're about, we need to look a little deeper into what is actually going on as we conduct this examination, our quality audit.

## The Activities of an Audit

As we analyze what actually goes on during a quality audit, we can come up with three primary activities of the auditor. They are:

- Gathering information
- Comparing information
- Asking why?

We'll talk about each of these aspects separately.

### Gathering information

There are hints of this activity within our working definition, but let's say it clearly and boldly right here and now, so there can be no mistake: auditors are information-gathering devices. Auditors are wound up and then go out and find out information about what is going on.

As information-gathering devices, we are blessed with some wonderful tools. It's always pleasant to discover that the tools we use as auditors are the same tools we use to survive. We use our senses, intelligence, and learning to survive, to get from day to day, to keep from starving, from being run-over in the street, from being alone. Our senses bring us information every second about our environment. We process that information quickly and sometimes, subtly, and it governs our actions. We *look* out at the sky to see if we want to carry an umbrella or not, we know to get out of the way when we *hear* a siren or *see* flashing red lights, we know when supper is about ready because we *smell* the food cooking. Our friends tell us things and ask us things and we respond based on what we *hear* and *understand* from them. We help an older person carry a heavy package because we *see* their need. We feel welcome or unwelcome by what we *see* or *feel* we see in someone else.

We are amazing and complex information gatherers and processors. It is necessary for our survival. It becomes even more essential as our world becomes faster and more complex. Our abilities to gather and process the appropriate level and types of information are more and more taxed. It is common to feel, these days, overload and to want to flee from the world, sit in a darkened room, listen to silence, not see or hear or feel much of anything. Sometimes deprivation may be essential to our sanity, but these times are the rare and infrequent moments. All the rest of the time, we need to absorb signs, gather information, process all we can absorb and gather so we can exist successfully.

What is interesting to note—particularly for neophyte auditors—is that being an auditor uses the same talents, skills, tools that we've used all our lives to get by, to survive, and to succeed. We don't have to go out and acquire new tools. We are like the character in the Moliere play who was delighted to realize that he could speak "prose." He goes around telling everyone that he can speak prose. To be an effective auditor means we gather information using our human tools. Heck, we've been doing that all along, anyway.

Quality auditors primarily use three information-gathering tools.

- Listening
- Observing
- Reading

Nothing new here, right? We have been listening and observing all of our lives and reading for most of them. Reading is the only acquired skill in the bunch. We can all learn to be better listeners and observers, but the fact that we have survived this long is a pretty good indication that we have been listening and observing effectively up to this point. Reading is something we had to learn how to do.

There may be some situations where other senses are used in quality auditing. Some years ago I had the opportunity to visit a large petrol-chemical plant where a sense of smell was required to determine the quality of the product. A sense of smell might be an important information-gathering tool in conducting an audit at that site. The same is true if an audit were being conducted in a restaurant, bakery, brewery, or a winery. A sense of taste might also be necessary in conducting such audits. But these are exceptions to the rule. Most of the time, the quality auditor is going to rely upon listening, observing, and reading skills.

Auditors begin gathering information from the moment they are given their audit assignments. Auditors have to base the audit on some written documentation, a standard or a procedure, something. In order to plan the audit, the auditor must learn about the organization, the process, the jobs to be audited, and that is done through reading. Generally, the product of the auditor's planning is some sort of document, call it a checklist or a plan, and that document is used during the audit. And the auditor gathers information about the organization, process, or job by reading documentation on site, from instructions to signs to records. It's all information.

## Comparing information

Once the information has been gathered, it is compared to something. In the definition of a quality audit, remember: *"...to determine if quality activities and related results comply with planned arrangements..."*? To determine compliance, a comparison must be made. In the case of a quality audit, the comparison is between the *"...quality activities and related results and the planned arrangements...."*

"Quality activities and related results" may be best translated into "what is going on" and proof of what has gone on. This is what the auditor is gathering information about. By reading, listening, and observing, the auditor is learning about what the organization is doing. By reviewing records the auditor learns what the results have been. Now the auditor compares that information with some set of known criteria, the "planned arrangements."

What did the organization plan to do? What was its intent? What did it say it was going to do?

The auditor finds this set of known criteria in different forms. It may be a standard the organization intends to comply with, or it may be in the organization's own documented system. There may be other forms of planned arrangements such as codes and regulatory requirements.

What is basic here is that the auditor is auditing the organization *to* something. There is some set of known criteria the organization should be performing to. We have all experienced situations where our performance has been criticized, and we discovered there was no criteria for performance. At least there was no stated one. It was all subjective, made up out of someone's head. Think of your anger. We were not audited to anything, or nothing that we were aware of.

The quality audit works from a base set of criteria, something to compare to.

## Finding out why

This is perhaps the most interesting aspect of auditing. It is the most demanding, the most challenging, the most difficult, and the most fun. It is also where value gets added to the audit process.

When the auditor finds a gap between what an organization is doing—the quality activities—and what it planned to do, or said it was going to do—the planned arrangements—the auditor tries to find out why the gap exists.

It's not that the auditor has to dig out the root cause of the gap. That's the organization's responsibility when it addresses corrective action. However, the auditor shouldn't just stop when the gap is found, write up the non-compliance and move on. This might not help the organization, and the auditor who does this misses so much.

Some years ago, I was conducting an audit in a small chemical plant. It is a common practice in chemical plants to take a sample of the final product and analyze the sample as proof the product meets requirements. It is also common to keep these samples and reports for a time should the customer require them. This company's procedure indicated they would retain these samples and the appropriate sample analysis reports for six months after the product left the plant. While auditing in the lab, where the sample records were kept, I found reports on file that were seven, eight, even nine months old. They were clearly not in compliance with their own procedure. A gap existed between what they said they were going to do and what they were actually doing. I could have stopped there and simply written up a noncompliance that *"...sample analysis reports are being kept longer than the procedure required..."* But the audit shouldn't stop there. At this point, there may be nothing but a small filing error. I had to dig a little deeper to confirm whether this was fact or not.

I collected a sample of three of the sample analysis reports which were out of compliance and went to the sample bin. This was a large wire cage where the actual product samples were stored in small bottles. I looked on the shelves and found the product samples corresponding to the reports.

So, I learned this wasn't a simple filing error.

The company was keeping samples and the records for longer than it said it would in its procedure.

My noncompliance was now: *"Samples and sample analysis reports are being kept for longer than the six months required by company procedure."*

But the trail is not ended. I still need to ask why.

I asked the woman who ran the lab why they were retaining samples and records for longer than six months. She explained to me that they often shipped their product to Europe and that it often didn't get into the customer's hands until six, seven, or more months had passed. They often got requests from their customers for samples and records eight and nine months after the product was shipped. They had to keep the samples and the records longer than six months.

See, they were being noncompliant on the side of the angels. They were actually doing the right thing for their business. They were still not in compliance with their procedure.

It was at this point I recorded the noncompliance. I had followed the trail to its logical conclusion. If I hadn't, if I had stopped at any spot along the trail and recorded my findings without continuing to dig, the company would have had to follow the same trail. I, also, would be unsure about how deep the problem went. Often the noncompliances discovered are only the tip of the iceberg. There's often a lot more buried under the sea. I wouldn't—and shouldn't—have been satisfied until I found the reason for the gap.

The gaps between what is happening, what has happened and what was supposed to have happened are where the real treasures lie in a quality audit. This is where the information the auditor and the company are seeking really is.

Let's say that an auditor is observing a machine operator perform a task. There is a set of detailed work instructions for this task, and the auditor is aware of these instructions. The operator is not following the instructions for the task and is performing the task in a different manner. At a simple level, there is a noncompliance, right? A gap between what was planned and what is happening, right? The auditor doesn't record the findings and go away. The auditor needs to find out why the gap exists. When the task is complete, the auditor interviews the operator. The first question might be if the operator is aware of the work instructions for this task.

Things could get interesting here.

The operator may get a quizzical look on his face and say simply, "Huh? What work instructions?"

If this happens, there is a possibility of a far more serious problem in this organization than just an operator not following instructions. It may be an indication that the quality system is not fully implemented. For any system to be effective it must be available to the users. If the users are not aware of it, then it is not available. The problem could be deep and serious. The auditor doesn't know this is true yet, but there is a trail to follow. The auditor might confirm this discovery by speaking to other operators performing the same task, then follow the trail back up through the system.

Let's say the auditor gets a different answer to the same question. Let's say the operator looks at the auditor and says, "Oh, yeah, I know about those instructions."

Now the auditor may ask, "Then why aren't you following them?"

The operator says something like, "Because they aren't right. Bob wrote them, he's the supervisor and he thinks he knows how to do this job, but he doesn't. If I followed the work instructions, I couldn't do the job right."

A totally different problem is indicated. Again, the problem may be more serious than an operator not following instructions. There may be a serious problem with the authenticity and correctness of the documented system. This may lead the auditor into a review of how the documents were created and how they were reviewed and approved.

Of course, the auditor should verify this indication by speaking with other operators performing the same task. It could be the auditor has stumbled on one of those stubborn individuals who isn't going to follow instructions, or someone who is going to find fault with any instructions. All the objective evidence the auditor has right now is that one operator is not following instructions.

Ah, but there are some tantalizing indications!

So much of auditing is good detective work. In another time, an auditor not interested in adding much value to the audit process would have simply written up the finding and went on his or her way. The company would have gotten notice of a noncompliance and would have taken corrective action. Depending on how good a job at corrective action the company did, the root cause for this problem may have been found and eliminated. But the auditor missed so many opportunities.

An experienced auditor once called this part of the auditing process as "...the continuing search for compliance." That has a nice positive ring to it, and I agree with it. Once a gap has been discovered, the auditor shouldn't be too quick to document the finding and move on. The auditor should dig deeper. There might be some important surprises there. Any auditor who doesn't dig deeper is not doing the company and the whole business of auditing full service.

Okay, we've looked at what goes on during an audit, but how do we do it?

## The Phases of an Audit

Audits have three major phases. They are:

- Planning
- Conducting
- Reporting

### Planning

Audit planning is all the activities the auditor does before he or she actually conducts the audit. Some of this is solitary, analytical, organizational effort, and some of it may involve initial interviews and planning sessions with the organization or person being audited. No matter, the purpose of the planning phase is to ensure the audit is complete, organized, and as successful as possible. Effective planning won't ensure a successful audit. There are too many factors involved in auditing for it to be that simple. However, ineffective planning will almost always guarantee an unsuccessful audit. The auditor who has not done effective planning will not get the required information and will appear slipshod and unprofessional.

### Conducting

The auditor conducts the audit according to the plan they have drawn up. The plan was drawn up to ensure the scope of the audit was covered. The plan directs the auditor's activities during the conduct of the audit. It is the guide. Now, the auditor is talking with people, listening to them, watching them work, reading additional pieces of information. This is the most interpersonal aspect of auditing. It is where the people skills are required, where interviewing techniques are applied, where good listening is essential, where alert observation is crucial.

There are differing opinions as to what is the most difficult of all the aspects of auditing. To a lot of new auditors this—conducting the audit—is the most difficult part. I could play devil's advocate and disagree. I have seen more difficulties in the recording and reporting the audit results. But I understand the difficulty. It is here where shyness and even a vestige of stage fright appears. Though we are all accomplished conversationalists, auditing is a focused conversation that requires concentration and alertness to nuance and subtlety. This is often what new auditors worry about the most. I realize the fear and trepidation, but I want to assure the new auditor of something. This is an evolving, growing set of skills. After every audit the auditor's response is that they missed something. They walk away wishing they had asked another question or a different question. They regret they were not able to establish enough rapport with the audit subject. No really successful auditor in my knowledge feels they have this aspect of auditing really nailed down. They are always improving their interviewing skills. So, to the new auditor I say, go ahead be worried, but always concentrate on improving. You can and you will.

## Reporting

My recent experiences have taught me that reporting on audits may be far more difficult than actually conducting them. While most of us are pretty good conversationalists, while we can even concentrate our focus on the interview, learn to ask the most effective questions, not all of us can write a noncompliance. Not all of us can record our observations clearly, concisely and precisely.

This is the part of auditing regarded as the most difficult. It may be because of the decline of reading and, especially, writing skills in the American population. It may also be simply embarrassment at our own writing skills. Whatever the problem, it is a very difficult aspect and one that we are going to spend a lot of time talking about later in this book.

We are going to follow this structure in this book. We will talk about how to plan an audit, how to conduct an audit according to that plan, and how to report on the results of an audit. Take a quick peek at the table of contents, if you have not done so already, and you will see the book follows this structure.

Before we start talking about the "how-to's," we need to get some more basic information out of the way.

## Categorizing Audits

It's human nature to categorize things as soon as we define them. And auditing is no different. There are many ways of categorizing audits, and many different names are used to identify different categories of audits. In this book we will talk about three ways of categorizing audits.

### Types of audits

A lot of publications and authorities will provide lists of different types of audits. Sometimes the items on the list are redundant, and sometimes they are misclassified and misunderstood. For our purpose, in the quality auditing world, there are really only two types of audits for us to be concerned with. As we define and explain the two types, you will see the quality activities being examined and the planned arrangements to be complied with are what is different. The two types of audits have different purposes and require different skills.

#### Adequacy

This type of audit determines if a documented system—or a part of a system—complies with the requirements of the standard, code, or regulation to which it is supposed to apply. For example, if a company is attempting to implement the ISO 9001 standard, a review of the company's documented quality system would tell the auditor if their system is "adequate."

Does it meet the requirements of the ISO 9001?

Sometimes this type of audit is called a "systems audit," or a "desk-top audit," or simply, "document review." Normally, this is a quiet audit, performed on the desk top, taking one person. A wag once noted that if you have any auditors who don't like to talk to people—a rare bird indeed— that they might be used to conduct a system audit or document review. The document is reviewed and compared, line by line, requirement by requirement, with the criteria it is supposed to match.

### Compliance

This type of audit measures the extent of compliance with a documented system or any set of criteria. This is the type of auditing we are most familiar with, where the auditor interviews people, reviews documents, and observes performance.

Are you doing what you said you were going to do? Are you complying?

The planned arrangements for this type of audit are, usually, the documented system.

During a formal assessment for registration to ISO 9001/2, both types of audits are performed. The registration agency firsts reviews the documented system to ensure the company's quality system meets the requirements of the applicable standard. Is it adequate? When the company's system is deemed adequate, auditors come to the company to ensure the company is complying to its system. The purpose of the audit is to ascertain that they are doing what they said they would do.

Most auditors within a company rarely get to do system audits or document review. However, they may be asked to review a new procedure to ensure it meets the requirements of the applicable standard, code, or regulation. In this case, the auditor would go to the requirement of the document and review it piece by piece, ensuring the procedure meets the requirements.

One variation of a compliance audit is a process audit. In a process audit, all aspects of a process are audited, but the auditor does not go outside that process. It may look like Figure 1–1:

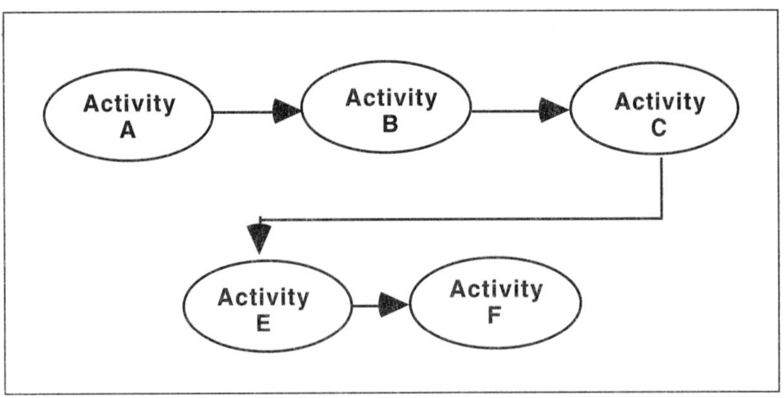


**Figure 1–1** Process audit

In the process audit, every aspect of the process is audited—from how orders get into the system to how the final product is delivered, but the audit does not go away from that process. A process audit can be very helpful in determining if all the parts of a system fit together. It is sort of auditing the white space between aspects of a quality system. Depending upon how you view it, a process audit is a very shallow, wide audit, or a very thin, narrow audit.

The product audit is another type of audit you may hear about. This is when a finished product is taken apart to determine if all components are present. Since this type of audit only deals with components and products, and not with the process, I have not included a discussion of it here. It is more of an inspection than an audit.

## Levels of audits

Another method of categorizing audits is by level, that is, who is auditing whom—or who is being audited. The magic number here is three.

### Internal

This is an organization examining itself, usually using its own resources. To put it in metaphysical terms, it is contemplating your own navel. Don't confuse this with the self-audit discussed earlier. Internal audits have to meet all audit criteria. That is, internal audits must be systematic and independent. Internal audits are carried out by personnel who do not have direct responsibility for the activity being audited.

### External

This is one organization examining another. Should an organization audit one of its suppliers, this would be an external audit. To continue with the metaphysical analogy, in an external audit the auditor is contemplating someone else's navel, which is often more fun than contemplating you own.

### Extrinsic

This is where an organization is being examined by another organization, someone else is contemplating your navel. This is an odd category to bring in—since the organization is not the actor, but the acted upon—but it is a common term that has grown up around the ISO world and is in common usage. When I first ran across this term I commented to the Englishman I was working with that we needed a new word. Extrinsic is not exactly in everyday usage in America. It is not in our idiom. He shrugged and said, "It's not the British idiom either." And look up "extrinsic" in the dictionary and it means "external." Just remember the organization is being acted upon from outside.

This will all get clearer when we talk about audit parties next.

## Audit parties

Another recent method of categorizing audits is by audit parties. Like the extrinsic classification above, this categorization may be of little use to us as auditors, but if we are in the ISO world in particular, it is important for us to understand the terms.

### First party

This is the internal audit. There is only party involved, the organization that is examining itself and its processes.

### Second party

In this type of audit there are two organizations involved, but the important fact is that the two organizations have a vested interest in each other. That is, they buy from or sell to each other. Should an organization audit its suppliers, those are second party, *external* audits. On the other hand, should a customer audit the organization as a supplier, that would be a second party, *extrinsic* audit. The important thing to remember is that each of the organizations have a vested interest in the quality system of the other.

### Third party

This audit introduces an outside, independent agency who neither buys the product or service nor sells a product or service to the organization being audited. In the ISO world, this agency is often referred to as "the third party registrar." But the same criteria exists outside the ISO world. Regulatory agencies are third parties, right? The key point to remember is that the third party audit is always done by an independent agency. All third party audits are *extrinsic*.

Because the relationships are different in each of these types of audits, the audits have minor wrinkles of difference when they are being conducted.

The internal audit may be a lot less formal, and the reporting of an internal audit may include elements missing from the others. After all, the auditor and the audited are all part of the same organization and share common goals.

A customer in a second party audit may have some particular areas of emphasis. For example, customers may spend a great deal of time during their audits looking into a company's control of suppliers.

Third party auditors have a goal of taking a comprehensive look at the entire system, so they tend not to emphasize one aspect of the system over another.

## Summary

During this chapter we have looked at some of the basic fundamentals of quality auditing.

- A working definition of a quality audit from ISO 8402
- What goes on during a quality audit
- The phases of a quality audit
- Some different methods of categorizing quality audits

# CHAPTER 2

# Quality Auditing and ISO 9000

## Introduction

Quality auditing is not a new thing on the horizon. It has been a fact of business for sometime. While it isn't new, there is a new interest in quality auditing that is reaching into all areas of business and touching almost everyone. There has also been some changes—an evolutionary plateau—in thinking about quality auditing. There has been a reexamining of the purpose of quality auditing, and there is renewed focus upon effective techniques and the overall effectiveness of auditing and auditors. So, while the subject may not be new, there are certainly enough new things around it to attract attention.

When I started this book, my intention was to address what I perceived as a quality auditing explosion. I had been working in parallel areas and was not subjected to quality audits until I started working in the quality arena. And I was exposed to a growth in this activity called quality auditing. I was impressed, and started to document what I thought was an explosion of auditing. The more I looked, the more I learned. It wasn't an explosion at all. All this auditing had been going on all the time under my nose. Well, there was a "bloomlet," but that wasn't the real story. The real story was the change in thinking about auditing. This was even more fascinating then an explosion. This was truly evolutionary.

What was once viewed as negative, at worst, or simply a nuisance, at best, was now being thought of in positive ways—as a partner in the effort to continuously improve the operation of an organization or a system within an organization. There were expanding qualifications for auditors. More was to be expected from auditors. More thought was being put into the results and the purpose of auditing and the kind of people who were going to audit.

I could be wrong in this, but I think the primary cause—or culprit, if you prefer—for this renewed interest in quality auditing was the introduction of the international quality management standard ISO 9000 to America in the late 80s. It was ISO 9000 that got me involved, and as application of this standard spread across the country, from area to area, business to business, like a wild fire, the new—evolutionary—thinking about quality auditing came along like fresh growth in the wake of the fire.

It is for this reason I decided to dedicate a chapter in this book to a discussion of ISO 9000. The ISO 9000 standard is interesting in its own right, but it is even more interesting in its use of auditing and the literature that has grown up around it about auditing.

If your organization is implementing ISO 9000, this book will be helpful. Then the techniques and tools in this book were designed and worked out in many successful ISO 9000 implementations. If your organization is not interested in applying ISO 9000, the book is still helpful. Everything in this book may be used with any type of quality auditing. Whether or not ISO 9000 is going to be implemented, the principles and concepts it supports are of value to quality auditors everywhere. So it is worth the investment.

## Background

ISO 9000 is a set of international quality management standards. It was developed and published by the International Organization for Standardization, which is headquartered in Geneva, Switzerland. The International Organization for Standardization was founded in 1946. It's mandate was to promote the worldwide standardization of products.

An example of this effort would be the effort to standardize the speeds of photographic film. Some years ago, in the U.S., we rated film speed by an ASA film speed rating—100, 200, 400, and so on. In the 60s we began to see another rating appear, the DIN rating. The DIN rating was German and it was used in Europe. We got a little table on the side of the film box that gave us both ratings. It doesn't take much to see the kind of madness this could lead to, with everyone having their own film speed rating. The hapless photographer would go mad trying to translate one speed rating into another, more familiar one. And the film manufacturers would have to put the film in a bigger box as the film speed rating table grew and grew.

Along comes the International Organization for Standardization. This organization comes up with a film speed rating system to be universally applied. This rating system is accepted worldwide. Now the manufacturer has only to put one rating on the box and the photographer only has to remember one rating, whether the film is bought in New York or in Beijing.

This is the International Organization for Standardization's mandate, and they have standardized product ratings and classifications all over the world. Now there are approximately 90 member countries in the organization, and the organization covers all areas except electronics and electrical engineering.

In the early 80s the organization formed a technical committee to design and develop a quality management standard that could be universally applied. The technical committee was designated TC176, and it was chaired by the Canadian representative on the committee. The U.S. representative on the committee was ASQC/ANSI (American Society for Quality Control and American National Standards Institute). This committee began its work by collecting and reviewing quality management standards from around the world.

Probably the two most influential sources for this effort were U.S. Military Standards and Specifications (MILSPECS) and British Standards (BS) for quality.

The U.S. had led the world up through World War II in the quality of its military equipment. It had managed to achieve this reputation through the rigorous application of military specifications.

The North Atlantic Treaty Organization (NATO) adopted the U.S. MILSPECs as the Allied Quality Assurance Publication(s) (AQAP) and applied them to gear and equipment for its forces.

The British adopted the AQAP as Defense Standards, or DEFSTANs, to be applied to equipment for Her Majesty's Forces. The British added a new wrinkle: design and development. Later, the British Department of Trade and Industry (DOTI) adopted the DEFSTANs for the civilian market, designating it British Standard (BS) 5750, and it was applied to all sorts of civilian industry in Great Britain.

It was these two standards—the U.S. MILSPECs and the British BS5750—that were to have the greatest impact upon the development of ISO 9000.

There were a couple of very large obstacles in TC176's way. One was that the quality management standard had to be pliable enough to be universally applied. It had to fit companies that produced a product as well as companies that provided a service. And it had to be applicable to companies of all sizes, from the huge down to the tiny. The second obstacle was that the standard had to be written so that it could be translated into other languages and retain the same meaning. This was no mean feat.

The original ISO 9000 family of standards was published in 1987. The British published a revised BS5750, which was aligned with the ISO 9000 series, and the Q90 series of standards was published in the U.S. The Q90 series Americanized the International English of the ISO standards, but the requirements were identical. Since then, the ISO 9000 standards were revised in 1992, and the revised version was published in 1994. In the U.S., the Q90 series was revised and reissued as the Q9000 series.

It is ISO 9000, 1994 that we are currently working with.

There are two principles in the ISO 9000 series of standards that are important to quality auditors. The first is that the standards reflect the most current thinking on quality. They are about *prevention* rather than detection. Until the 80s the operational thrust of quality standards was inspection. They were largely maps for inspection systems. The idea was that quality could be inspected into the product. This changes with ISO 9000. The dictum now is: *let's create a system that builds quality into the product, and let's monitor that system. In this manner we can prevent defects from ever occurring.*

When quality was about inspections, it was largely the business of a quality department, and a quality manager, and a crew of inspectors.

Now, since quality is about prevention and process, it is *everyone's* business.

The second principle that impacts on quality auditors is that a system of internal auditing was required by the ISO 9000 standards. So quality system auditing became an integral part of ensuring compliance and for providing on-going maintenance of the system.

Incidentally, ISO does not stand for the organization that developed and published the standard. It is the not the initials of the International Organization for Standardization. ISO is derived from a Greek word, and is translated to mean "equal" or "level." It is pronounced "Eye-So" and not "Eye-Ess-Oh."

Okay, that is a little something of where the standard came from. Now, let's look at the standard itself.

## The ISO 9000 Family of Documents

We are often very careless in our speech. We often refer to "ISO 9000" as all or anyone of the documents that make up the family. We say, "Oh, we're implementing ISO 9000," or "We just got registered to ISO 9000." We ought to be more careful.

ISO 9000 is a *family* of documents. The title ISO 9000 can refer to both an individual document and to the family. The core ISO 9000 family has five members. They are shown in Table 2–1.

It is proper to refer to the "ISO 9000 family of documents," meaning all of the documents that make up the ISO

**Table 2–1** The ISO 9000 Family of Documents

| ISO 9000 | ISO 9001 | ISO 9002 | ISO 9003 | ISO 9004 |
|---|---|---|---|---|
| Quality management and quality assurance standards - Part 1: Guidelines for selection and use | Quality systems - Model for quality assurance in design, development, production, installation and servicing | Quality systems - Model for quality assurance in production, installation and servicing | Quality systems - Model for quality assurance in final inspection and test | Quality management and quality system elements - Part 1: Guidelines |
| no requirements | 20 requirements | 19 requirements | 16 requirements | no requirements |

9000 standard. It is also proper to refer to the first of the family of documents as "ISO 9000." Let's look at the five immediate family members closely.

- ISO 9000—The specific document, ISO 9000, is not an *operable standard*. It has no requirements to be met. The original ISO 9000, now called "-1", was created to be a guideline to assist companies in selecting which of the operable standards to implement. The key point to remember about ISO 9000 is that it is a *guideline*. It says so in the title. And a guideline is simply that. It isn't mandatory.

  Since its initial publication, ISO 9000 has grown into a significant subfamily of documents on its own, giving guidelines for not just the application of the standard but also for particular industries.

- ISO 9001—this is the first of the *operable standards*. It is the most comprehensive of the three operable standards. It has 20 requirements and includes the design and development function.

- ISO 9002—the second of the *operable standards*, this standard has 19 requirements and covers companies who produce products or offer services, who install their products/services and who provide service for their products/services. The only difference between ISO 9002 and ISO 9001 is the control of the design and development process, paragraph 4.4.

- ISO 9003—the third *operable standard,* is not widely used or applied these days. It covers those companies who do nothing but final inspection and test. Usually, if this is what a company does, it is regarded as a service, and, therefore, fits under ISO 9002. Not many companies are being registered to this operable standard, and there is a rumor that it might disappear altogether.
- ISO 9004—a look at the title of this document tells you it is not an operable standard. There is the key word "guidelines." This lets us know it is not an operable standard. The best description of ISO 9004 came from a British friend of mine who called it, "...a philosophical treatise on the nature of quality systems...." That's a pretty apt description. Like ISO 9000, this document has spawned its own subfamily of guideline documents. There are something like seven of them at this writing.

Other family members have joined the ISO 9000 family and we need to say something about them here.

- ISO 8402 Quality Vocabulary
  This is a small dictionary with the ISO definitions for commonly used terms, such as "quality" and "quality audits."
- ISO 10011, Parts 1, 2 and 3
  These are a set of guidelines, published in 1990, to describe the conduct of audits, qualification criteria for auditors and lead auditors, and management of audit programs. We will be revisiting these guidelines later.

## ISO 9001/2—The Operable Standards

As was pointed out earlier, two key principles in the ISO 9000 family of standards are (1) they are about prevention rather than detection and (2) they involve everyone (or virtually everyone) in quality. Let's take a quick trip around one of the operable standards to see how these principles work.

Open up either ISO 9001 or 9002 and you will quickly see the requirements are very comprehensive in terms of an organization's business. Here is a list of the requirements for ISO 9001, the most comprehensive of the operable standards (Table 2–2):

**Table 2–2** Requirements of ISO 9001

| ISO 9001—4.0 Quality System Requirements | |
|---|---|
| 4.1 Management Responsibility | 4.11 Control of Inspection, Measuring, and Test Equipment |
| 4.2 Quality System | 4.12 Inspection and Test Status |
| 4.3 Contract Review | 4.13 Control of Non-Conforming Product |
| 4.4 Design Control | 4.14 Corrective and Preventive Action |
| 4.5 Document and Data Control | 4.15 Handling, Storage, Packaging, Preservation, and Delivery |
| 4.6 Purchasing | 4.16 Control of Quality Records |
| 4.7 Control of Customer Supplied Product | 4.17 Internal Quality Audits |
| 4.8 Product Identification and Traceability | 4.18 Training |
| 4.9 Process Control | 4.19 Servicing |
| 4.10 Inspection and Testing | 4.20 Statistical Techniques |

These requirements are very easy to apply to a business, if we use a typical, generic business cycle.

### Customer order

A customer orders the product or the service the company makes or provides. This is covered by paragraph 4.3 of the standard, which is about ensuring the company understands exactly what the customer wants.

### Design and design verification/validation

If the product or service is or requires design, the company plans, designs, and develops the design. This includes the verification and the validation of the design. This is covered by paragraph 4.4 of the standard.

### Resources (including equipment, material and personnel)

To produce this product, or to provide this service, the company may have to purchase equipment (4.9) or materials (4.6) or it may have to identify, hire, and train people (4.9, 4.18).

### Production

The production must be planned and carried out under controlled conditions. This is covered by paragraphs 4.8 and 4.9 of the standard.

### Inspection and testing

Some sort of verification activities are planned and carried to ensure the product meets requirements (4.10). The equipment used for inspection, measuring and testing equipment is controlled (4.11), and the status of the product—whether it passed or failed—is clearly identified (4.12).

### Storage and shipping

The product is stored and is shipped to the customer. This is covered in paragraph 4.15.

### Servicing

The company may offer after-sales servicing as part of the initial contract, paragraph 4.19.

To support this cycle there are a lot of mechanisms that may impact anywhere on the cycle. They are:

### Management Responsibility (Paragraph 4.1)

Management's role in defining objectives and commitment, in defining authority and responsibility, in providing resources and in reviewing the system to ensure that it is still what is required.

### The Quality System (Paragraph 4.2)

A documented system that defines the processes the company needs in order to conduct its business.

### Document and Data Control (Paragraph 4.5)

If there is a documented system, then it must be controlled to ensure that people are using the correct documents.

### Control of Customer Supplier Product (Paragraph 4.7)

If and when the customer gives the company anything that goes into the final product, how it is verified and maintained and controlled.

### Control of the Non-Conforming Product (Paragraph 4.13)

When and if there is nonconforming product—at any stage—how is it identified so that it is not inadvertently used, and what does the company do with this nonconforming product (disposition).

### Corrective and Preventive Action (Paragraph 4.14)

How the company corrects problems and prevents their reoccurrence, and how the company prevents problems from ever happening in the first place.

### Control of Quality Records (Paragraph 4.16)

At most every stage in the cycle a record is created as proof that the process was followed and the results were satisfactory. How does the company maintain these records?

### Internal Quality Audits (Paragraph 4.17)

The company has to establish and operate a program of audits (usually using its own resources) to determine compliance with the system and to provide information about the need to change—improve—the system.

### Training (Paragraph 4.18)

The company must identify its training needs, provide for the necessary training, and keep appropriate training records.

### Statistical Techniques (Paragraph 4.20)

If statistical techniques are appropriate, the company must decide how and where they are going to be used.

As I said at the beginning of this little tour, this book is not about ISO 9000, but this international standard is worth a quick study for its impact upon quality and quality systems. From this quick look at the ISO standard you can see how comprehensive it is. It touches almost every aspect of a business, but there is one aspect that is especially important to us and our purpose in this book.

## The Internal Audit Requirement

What is really the key to our discussion here is how the ISO 9000 standards require an internal audit program. The requirement for an internal audit program is in each of the operable standards—ISO 9001, 9002, and 9003—and it is fundamentally identical.

Simply because the ISO 9000 requirement is a good, well-written one, and because other standards that have come along after have borrowed from it, let's take a little time and look at it some detail (Table 2–3).

This is the basic ISO 9000 requirement, identical in ISO 9001 and 9002. It requires that there be a system of internal audits, that the auditors be independent, that there be a schedule, that the results be documented and shared with the people being audited, that there be corrective action, and that there be some kind of follow-up activity to see the corrective action was taken and that it was effective.

**Table 2–3** The ISO 9000 Internal Audit Requirement

| ISO Requirement | Key Points |
|---|---|
| 4.17 Internal quality audits | |
| The supplier shall establish and maintain documented procedures for planning and implementing internal quality audits to verify whether quality activities and related results comply with planned arrangements and to determine the effectiveness of the quality system. | • The *supplier* is your company<br>• *Shall* is a mandatory requirement<br>• Must have a documented procedure for internal audits<br>• *To verify* compliance<br>• *To determine* effectiveness of the system—is it working? |
| Internal quality audits shall be scheduled on the basis of the status and importance of the activity to be audited and shall be carried out by personnel independent of those having direct responsibility for the activity being audited. | • Internal audits must be *scheduled*<br>• Scheduled on the basis of *status* and *importance*<br>• Auditors must be *independent* |
| The results of the audits shall be recorded (see 4.16) and brought to the attention of the personnel having responsibility in the area being audited. The management personnel responsible for the area shall take timely corrective action on the deficiencies found during the audit. | • Results of audit is a quality record<br>• Must inform personnel having responsibility in area<br>• Management must take timely corrective action |
| Follow-up activities shall record the implementation and effectiveness of the corrective action taken (see 4.16). | • Follow-up activities record corrective action<br>• This is also a quality record |

There was one word from the 1987 version of the ISO standard that was deleted in the 1994 version, and that word was "comprehensive." It used to read that the company had to have a comprehensive system of internal audits. What was clear in the use of the word comprehensive was that the audit had to cover all aspects of the system. Why it was dropped, I have no idea.

But it isn't enough to run a system of internal audits simply because the ISO 9000 standard requires it. It's that type of lock-step thinking that causes vast, ineffective bureaucracies and gives systems a bad name. Audits should be an integral part of any quality system. The reason why is contained within the requirement itself:

> *"...to verify whether quality activities and related results comply with planned arrangements and to determine the effectiveness of the quality system."*

Internal quality audits are conducted to verify if the company is complying with its documented quality system (Is everyone doing what our system says they should be doing?) and, also, to provide information so the company can determine if its quality system is effective (Is the quality system helping the company achieve its objectives?)

This is very clear once we look further into the ISO 9000 standard and other requirements that relate to the internal audit program. Corrective action is mentioned directly, and at the end of the requirement for the internal audit program there is a note. Notes in the ISO 9000 standard are guidelines and are not mandatory requirements, but this note is very telling. It reads:

> *"The results of internal quality audits form an integral part of the input to management review activities (see 4.1.3)"*

So in understanding the audit program we need to consider paragraph 4.14, Corrective and Preventive Action, and paragraph 4.1.3, Management Review.

## Corrective Action

Corrective action for problems found during the audit is mandated in the internal audit requirement.

> *"The management personnel responsible for the area shall take timely corrective action on the deficiencies found during the audit."*

The requirement puts the responsibility for corrective action squarely on the shoulders of management personnel. This is where it ought to be, because even though nonmanagement personnel may guide and be a part of the determination for corrective action and may even carry it out, and see it is effectively implemented, it is a management responsibility.

A particularly interesting thing to note is that the standard mentions nothing about the severity of the deficiencies found during the audit. It states there must be corrective action taken for all deficiencies.

Let's review paragraph 4.14 (Table 2–4).

**Table 2–4** Corrective and Preventive Action

| ISO Requirement | Key Points |
|---|---|
| **4.14 Corrective and preventive action**<br>**4.14.1 General**<br>The supplier shall establish and maintain documented procedures for implementing corrective and preventive action. | • The *supplier* is your company<br>• *Shall* is a mandatory requirement |

**Table 2–4** Corrective and Preventive Action (continued)

| ISO Requirement | Key Points |
|---|---|
| Any corrective or preventive action taken to eliminate the causes of actual or potential nonconformities shall be to a degree appropriate to the magnitude of problems and commensurate with the risks encountered. | • Must have documented procedures for implementing corrective and preventive action<br>• Corrective and preventive actions are appropriate and commensurate |
| The supplier shall implement and record any changes to the documented procedures resulting from corrective and preventive action. | • Must implement and record changes to procedures |
| **4.14.2 Corrective Action**<br>The procedures for corrective action shall include: | |
| a) the effective handling of customer complaints and reports of product nonconformities; | • Customer complaints and reports of product nonconformities |
| b) investigation of the cause of nonconformities relating to product, process and quality system, and recording the results of the investigation (see 4.16); | • Causes investigated and record kept |
| c) determination of the corrective action needed to eliminate the cause of nonconformities; | • Corrective action determined |
| d) application of controls to ensure that corrective action is taken and that it is effective. | • Controls to ensure corrective action has been taken and that it is effective |
| **4.14.3 Preventive action**<br>The procedures for preventive action shall include: | |
| a) the use of appropriate sources of information such as processes and work operations which affect product quality, concessions, audit results, quality records, service reports and customer complaints to detect, analyze and eliminate potential causes of nonconformities; | • Analyze information about system and system performance to eliminate potential causes |

**Table 2–4** Corrective and Preventive Action (continued)

| ISO Requirement | Key Points |
|---|---|
| b) determination of the steps needed to deal with any problems requiring preventive action; | • Actions determined |
| c) initiation of preventive action and application of controls to ensure that it is effective; | • Initiation of action and application of controls |
| d) ensuring the relevant information on actions taken is submitted for management review (see 4.1.3). | • Report to management |

Again, you see there is no degree of severity noted in this requirement. *All* nonconformities require corrective action. There is no requirement for major and minor nonconformities. (We'll discuss this issue later.)

Also, note, the corrective action process is clearly spelled out: investigate, determine, implement and ensure effectiveness. There is no allowance for quick fix. The causes of the nonconformity must be investigated, the corrective action must be implemented, and there should be some evidence the determined corrective action was taken and that it was effective.

It is in preventive action that internal audits are mentioned. After analysis and determination of preventive action, there is a requirement to submit information to management for review. This is the second reference to management review we have come across, so let's review the management review requirement.

## Management Review

This is a very important and interesting paragraph (Table 2–5). At once, it reaffirms management commitment to the quality system, which is one of the critical aspects of the ISO 9000 standards. These standards are very strong about ensuring that management is aware of its responsibility for an effective quality system by giving management certain specific tasks. (At least one accreditation agency believes management responsibility is so important that its procedures for assessment require that one of the assessment team audit it as soon as the assessment begins.)

**Table 2-5** Management review

| Key Points | ISO Requirement |
|---|---|
| **4.3.1 Management review**<br>The supplier's management with executive responsibility shall review the quality system at defined intervals sufficient to ensure its continuing suitability and effectiveness in satisfying the requirements of this International Standard and the supplier's stated quality policy and objectives (see 4.1.1). Records of such reviews shall be maintained (see 4.16). | • The *supplier* is management with executive responsibility<br>• *Shall* is a mandatory requirement<br>• Defined intervals<br>• Ensures suitability and effectiveness<br>• Records kept |

So, who should conduct, or be directly involved with management review? "The supplier's management with executive responsibility..." The easiest definition of "...management with executive responsibility..." is "top management," top management for the *scope* of the system. If it is a corporate system, top management is corporate chief executive officer (CEO); if the system is site specific, top management may be the plant manager. A little detective work will demonstrate how we arrived at this conclusion.

- The first time in the ISO 9000 standards where the term, "...supplier's management with executive responsibility...," appears, is in regards to the quality policy, paragraph 4.1.1.

> *"The supplier's management with executive responsibility shall define and document its policy for quality, including objectives for quality and its commitment to quality."* (emphasis added)

- In the Quality Vocabulary publication, ISO 8402, quality policy is defined as:

  > *"The overall quality intentions and direction of an organization as regards quality, as formally expressed by top management."* (emphasis added)

- Thus, it is clear the person or persons conducting or playing a part in management review is top management.

So, the ISO 9000 standards require that top management review the quality system at defined intervals. Notice, the standard doesn't define the intervals. It only states the interval should be *"...sufficient to ensure its (the quality system's) continuing suitability and effectiveness to achieve objectives."*

What objectives is the paragraph referring to?

The objectives as stated in the company's quality policy! Remember, in the passage quoted above, the requirement was for a documented quality policy that had the company's *objectives* for and *commitment* to quality. Management reviews the quality system to see if it is helping the company achieve its objectives. The results of internal audit are an integral part of this review. The information that internal auditors generate and record are essential to determine the effectiveness of the quality system.

## System Maintenance

What is clear from this brief standard review is the importance and value of the audit program, but, also, something bigger is beginning to emerge. There is a mechanism for continuous process improvement imbedded in the ISO 9000 standards. I call this mechanism "system maintenance."

We have all suffered under systems that couldn't be easily changed, that didn't have a mechanism for change, improvement, within their workings. Often we shake our heads at the working of government for exactly this reason: the seeming impossibility of change. The people who developed the ISO 9000 standards realized this, so they built mechanisms within the standards so that systems created to meet their requirements would never become stagnant.

## Internal audits

The internal audit system itself is a very important system maintenance mechanism. The following figure shows (Figure 2–1) the internal audit process.

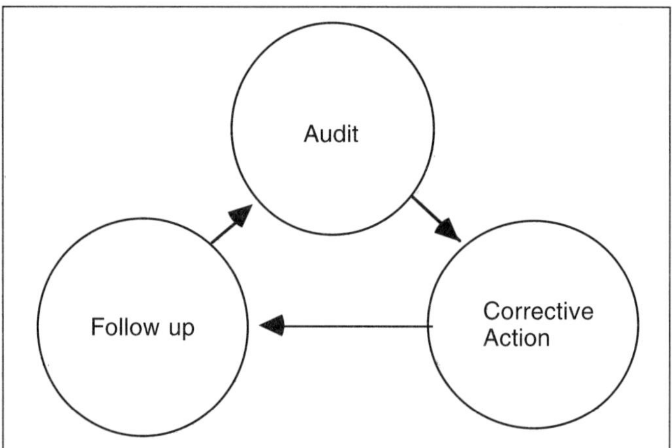


**Figure 2–1** The audit-corrective action-follow-up triangle

As nonconformities are discovered during internal audits, corrective actions are taken. Corrective action, as you recall, requires investigation, determination of action, and controls to ensure the corrective action is taken. The internal audit paragraph requires some sort of follow-up action be taken to ensure that corrective action has been taken and that it is effective.

## Other important system maintenance mechanisms

Internal audits aren't the only method the organization has for maintaining and improving its system. There are others.

- Document control—control of the documented system also means encouraging changes to the system, when required. The document control procedure contains the method for changing, and improving, system documents.
- The registration process—when an organization decides to become registered, it hires an outside registration company to assess its system and its compliance to its system. This registration is normally good for three years, and during that three years, the registration agency continually assesses the company's compliance. This is a working partnership that results in continuous process improvement.

## The internal audit-management review-corrective action triangle

By far the most important mechanism for maintaining the system is the internal audit-management review-corrective action system. If we were to diagram this system, it might look like Figure 2-2.

The internal audit program—though the nonconformities discovered during the audits are corrected and followed up—provides information to the management team for review. The management review team decides if the quality system is helping the company achieve its objectives—as stated in the quality policy—and enacts corrective action when it is not. This keeps the system alive and growing, and improving.

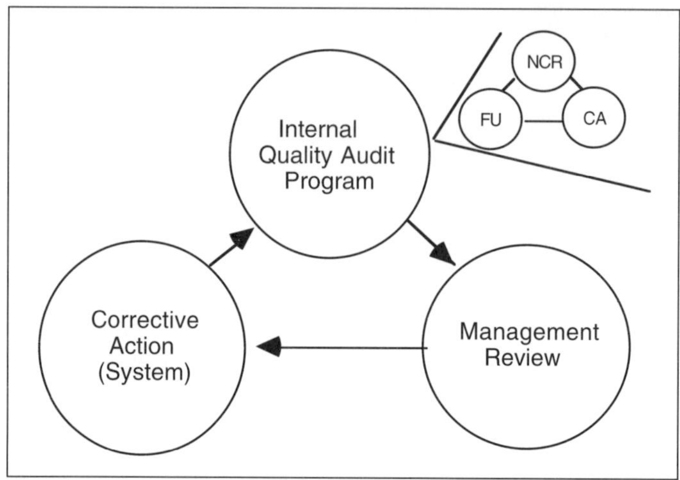


**Figure 2–2** Audit-management review-corrective action

## Summary

The widespread application of the ISO 9000 standards has caused an explosion in auditing in the American business community. Although this handbook is not expressively for the ISO 9000 standard internal audit program or auditor, the ISO 9000 standard offers a good model for the design and operation of an internal auditing program.

# CHAPTER 3

# The Quality Auditor

## Introduction

Whatever you may think of auditors and auditing, there is one central fact you should keep in mind: auditing is fundamentally a human activity. You've been doing it, in one way or another, for as long as you have been alive. How good an auditor you are can be judged by how successful you have navigated your world up to this point. We all know people who are accident prone, who are always in the wrong place at the wrong time, and it easy to classify them as being not very good auditors. Good auditors are alert and aware. They see what is going on around them. They hear what is happening. They analyze all the sensory inputs and chart a course that avoids the dangers and the pitfalls. They navigate successfully based on the collection of information and an accurate analysis of it.

The quality audit is a tightened knot of time—an analysis of a particular event or activity—demanding a heightened concentration of our alertness, awareness, and of our analytical skills. It is a compression of those skills and abilities we use to constantly—successfully—navigate our way through life.

Doesn't sound like too much fun so far, does it? Well, read on.

Auditing is hard work. It is difficult and demanding. Since it is a compression of our abilities and skills, it demands great planning and concentration to bring off successfully. It also taxes a variety of skills. The effective auditor must be a thorough planner, an organizer, an interviewer, and writer. A wide range of skills to be sure, and all of them are essential to be an effective auditor.

It is also kind of like swimming against the tide sometimes. Until people really understand the auditor's relationship to the successful operation of a quality system, the auditor is often viewed as a nuisance or an enemy.

It is also an evolutionary activity. There is no such thing as a perfect audit or auditor. We are all just working at trying to get better. That's the principle behind this book, any auditor training you take, and any self-evaluation and improvement program you might do. Knowing that auditing is a journey rather than a destination gives us a place to start, a beginning.

No, I'm not trying to turn people away from becoming quality auditors. Auditing is challenging and rewarding. It is one of the greatest learning activities in which you'll ever be involved. The amount of technical knowledge you will gain over time will astound you, but, more importantly, the insights you will gain into human character and activity will be even greater.

With this sense of enthusiasm and challenge, let's start with a definition of what an auditor is.

## The Quality Auditor

Remember back in high school when you drove a teacher crazy by defining something by just repeating yourself? The International Organization of Standardization, the folks who brought us the ISO standards, are guilty of this kind of double-speak. In their publication ISO 10011-1, *Guidelines for Auditing Quality Systems—Part 1—Auditing*, they define a quality auditor in the following fashion:

> **3.3 auditor (quality):**
> a person who has the qualification to perform quality audits

That's all you know and all you need to know.

Actually, it's not. For our purposes we need to try to get hold of this slippery creature, the auditor, if for no other reason than to fully understand what is expected of us.

We can use the ISO 10011 definition as a starting place, and by the end of this chapter, I hope, you will be able to define, to sketch a picture of the auditor. A self-portrait, perhaps? Let's make that the goal of this chapter, and let's begin by looking at what the auditor's responsibilities are. Perhaps if we can define the role—what is expected of us—we might be better able to define ourselves.

## ISO 10011

ISO 10011-1 is the first of three guidelines published by the International Organization for Standardization to assist auditors and audit program managers in understanding their roles in the ISO 9000 world. They contain a lot of good information and can serve as guidelines in all of quality auditing efforts.

The three 10011 guidelines are shown in Table 3–1.

**Table 3–1** ISO 10011 Guidelines

| ISO 10011-1 | ISO 10011-2 | ISO 10011-3 |
|---|---|---|
| Guidelines for auditing quality systems— Part 1: *Auditing* | Guidelines for auditing quality systems — Part 2: *Qualification criteria for quality systems auditors* | Guidelines for auditing quality systems— Part 3: *Management of audit programs* |

It is in ISO 10011-1 that we find a discussion of the roles and responsibilities of audit teams, auditors and lead auditors, so let's begin there.

## The audit team

It is not uncommon, even on internal audits, for an audit to be conducted by a team of auditors. These teams may be structured a couple of ways.

In the most common use of teams, the individual team members conduct their audits alone, and come back together with the other team members to discuss findings and put together the final report.

Sometimes the audits themselves are conducted by a team. The greatest benefit to this kind of team approach is that there is a better chance to get coverage of the entire audit scope. It is also a little easier on the individual auditors. One can be taking notes and preparing the next series of questions while another is conducting a part of the interview. For this reason, it is often favored with novice auditors.

The major drawback is that team audits take at least twice as many people. Instead of tying up one person to conduct the audit, there are at least two people involved. There is another drawback, and that is the possible intimidation factor. Sometimes a team may seem to be ganging up on the person being audited. It can get a little intimidating for them.

Most audit teams work as a team to plan, discuss, and report on the results, but conduct the audits individually. The individual auditors collect their evidence and bring it to the team. The team reviews it and discusses it. The team hashes over the findings, disputing the evidence, keeping each other honest and sharp. Errors are discovered, and incomplete evidence is caught.

Whenever the audit is conducted as a team, one of the people on the team should be designated the team leader for the audit and should be responsible for the activities of a lead auditor.

## Audits and assessments

This is as good a time as any to clear up some confusion dealing with the words audit and assessment. Often, we use the words interchangeably, and this doesn't help our confusion. Our British friends have a very valid method of separating the two terms. I think if we use their definitions of the terms we'll be better off.

- An *audit* is an examination of a single activity, department, job, or so forth. The audit develops a snap-shot in time for that particular activity, department, job, whatever.
- An *assessment* is a collection and collation of audits. Assessments are carried on by teams, and each member of the team conducts audits. The assessment is the collection of those separate audits. If we continue with the photo analogy, the assessment is a photo album.

For some reason, here in America we have confused the issue even more. In England the person who is registered to manage teams and conduct assessments is called a Lead Assessor. In America we refer to this person as a Lead Auditor. You figure!

## The auditor's responsibilities

Below is a listing—and discussion—of the auditor's responsibilities as outlined in ISO 10011-1.

The auditor is responsible for:

- *"...complying with the applicable audit requirements..."* At the beginning of every audit a purpose and scope should be clearly stated and given to the auditor. It may be given by the team leader or by the manager of the audit program. The auditor must completely understand the audit's purpose and scope. It is the auditor's responsibility to work within this purpose and scope. The criteria—the "planned arrangements"—should be clearly identified, and the auditor should plan the audit based on these criteria. Also, the audit should be conducted in accordance with documented procedures. The auditor is responsible for understanding his or her role in this particular audit process.
- *"...communicating and clarifying audit requirements..."* There should be no mystery to auditing. The people being audited are often intimidated enough by the very fact they are being audited. The auditor must overcome this obstacle to free and open communication. One of the methods to overcome this obstacle is by demystifying the process. The auditor should communicate the audit's purpose and scope, should obtain agreement on the criteria to be used, and should be prepared to answer any questions about the process.
- *"...planning and carrying out assigned responsibilities effectively and efficiently..."*

Yes, this makes sense, doesn't it? The auditor is responsible for his or her part in the process. Conducting a successful audit means good planning, getting the information, and doing everything effectively and efficiently. Later in this book we're going to talk about planning, conducting and reporting on an audit, and you'll get some practical guidelines in how to meet these responsibilities as well as some tools to help you.

- *"...documenting the observations..."*
  If you remember back to our discussion of the ISO 9000 standards, you will recall that we said: *"The results of the audit shall be recorded..."* This simply means the auditor must document what he or she found during the audit. This places demands on your writing skills. It is deceptively simple, and yet one of the most difficult aspects of auditing.

- *"...reporting the audit results..."*
  The ISO 9000 standards continued on about the documented results of the audit: *"...and brought to the attention of responsible personnel in the area being audited."* Not only does the auditor have to document the findings, he or she must also report the results. In an individual audit this means discussing your findings with the person being audited and getting their acknowledgment. In team audits it means giving a presentation of your results.

- *"...verifying the effectiveness of corrective actions taken as a result of the audit (if requested)..."*
  While it is not, traditionally, the auditor's responsibility to recommend corrective action, there may be times when the auditor is asked to perform follow-up activities to ensure that corrective action has been taken and that it has been effective. This may mean reviewing documented evidence of corrective action. It could also

mean conducting a second audit to verify implementation and effectiveness.

- *"...retaining and safeguarding documents pertaining to the audit..."*
  Audits reveal nonconformities—places and instances where the quality system is not being complied with—and this is information that is best regarded as sensitive. The auditor is responsible for guarding the confidentiality of the documents and information about the audit and its results. This includes:
  (1) submitting the documents as required;
  (2) ensuring the confidentiality;
  (3) treating all privileged information with discretion.
- *"...cooperating with and supporting the lead auditor..."*
  We will look at the responsibilities of the team leader on the next pages, but here it should be emphasized the team leader has the overall responsibility for the conduct of the entire audit. To ensure success, each auditor must cooperate with and support the team leader.

These are the responsibilities of the auditor as defined in ISO 10011-1. A quick review of them will confirm the demands placed upon the individual auditor.

## The team leader

Since there is a difference in the use of the titles lead auditor and lead assessor, I have decided to stick with the neutral, I hope, term team leader. Whatever you call this person, he or she is the auditor in charge of the audit team. The team leader's responsibilities are:

- *...the overall responsibility for all phases of the audit."*

The team leader should be a person with management capabilities and some experience. The team leader has the authority—and the responsibility—to make final decisions regarding the conduct of the audit.

- *"...assisting with the selection of other team members..."*
  Sometimes the team leader has the sole responsibility for selecting the members of the team, and sometimes the selection is done in conjunction with the organization requesting the audit. However it is done, the team leader has the responsibility to ensure the correct kind and number of auditors are selected for the job.

- *"...preparation of the audit plan..."*
  This is the overall plan for the entire audit, including the selection of areas to be audited, the assignment of team members and the internal schedule of events.

- *"...representing the audit team with the auditee's management..."*
  The team leader is the point of contact during a team audit. Should the organization or activity being audited have any problems with the auditors or the team, it should bring this up with the team leader.

- *"...submitting the audit report..."*
  Audit team members contribute information and data to the audit report, but the report of the audit is the team leader's responsibility. Now, this does not necessarily mean the team leader writes the report. Someone on the team who, perhaps, has better expertise at putting word on paper may actually do the report, but it is the team leader's responsibility.

All of this gives us a pretty good picture of what is expected of the auditor, but let's dig a little deeper into what the activities of the auditor are.

## The team leader's activities

If you ever find yourself acting in the role of a team leader, here are your activities. The team leader should:

- *"...define the requirements for each assignment, including the required auditor qualifications..."*
  The team leader puts the team together. The team leader selects team members based on the requirements of the audit, and then defines what each of the team members are responsible for.
- *"...comply with applicable auditing requirements and other appropriate directives..."*
  The team leader is responsible for seeing that team members comply with the requirements of the audit and any protocol associated with it.
- *"...plan the audit, prepare working documents and brief the audit team..."*
  Each member will plan their own audits, but the team leader is responsible for the overall planning.
- *"...review documentation on existing quality system activities to determine their adequacy..."*
  This is the adequacy audit, or document review. The team leader is responsible for seeing that this audit gets done.
- *"...report critical nonconformities to the auditee immediately..."*
  This is particularly important during a registration audit where the criticalities of nonconformities are categorized for the benefit of advising registration or not. This is not as critical in first- or second-party audits, because the nonconformities are not categorized in these audits.
- *"...report any major obstacles encountered in performing the audit..."*
  Remember, it is the team leader's responsibility to be the contact with the people/organization being audited.

If a team member encounters problems, the member should bring the problems to the team leader's attention as soon as possible.

- *"...report on the audit results clearly, concisely and with undue delay..."*
  Reporting on team audits is the responsibility of the team leader. The individual team members usually present their findings, and all the findings of the audit form the audit report. The team leader is responsible for submitting the audit report.

So, that covers the activities of the team leader, what about the auditor?

## The auditor's activities

The auditor should:

- *"...remain within the scope.."* of the audit.
  This is sometimes very difficult for auditors to do, especially neophyte auditors, and it is sometimes a trick played on auditors by the organization being audited. They will lead the auditor astray, outside of his or her scope. The auditor must stay within the scope, that is what the audit plan the team leader has created requires.
- *"...exercise objectivity..."*
  It is why we have been stressing independence. The auditor needs to be as objective as he or she can be. It is not the auditor's job to tell the auditee that their system is wrong. It is the auditor's job to tell the auditee that the system is not being followed or used. This takes objectivity on the part of the auditor.
- *"...collect and analyze evidence that is relevant and sufficient to permit the drawing of conclusions regarding the audited quality system..."*

This the actual conduct of the audit. The auditor observes, listens, reads, gathers information, and analyzes and records it. As we pointed out, the auditor is an information gathering device. We are wound up and sent out to gather information.

- *"...remain alert to any indications of evidence that can influence the audit results and possibly require more extensive auditing..."*
  Events are spinning around the auditor all the time, and the effective auditor is keen of what is happening around them. There is always a chance that some small event—maybe unnoticed by most people—may point a way down an audit trail that may, otherwise, have remained hidden.
- *"...act in an ethical manner at all times..."*
  The auditor must be ethical in dealing with the audit population and the members of their team

All this information gives us some insight into what the auditor is responsible for and what the auditor actually does, and this is all valuable if we are to build an image in our mind of what an auditor should be.

## Defining the Role

Before you are asked to play a role, you should have an understanding of it. This is why we have reviewed what ISO 10011 says about the auditor's activities and responsibilities. We still may not have enough of a feel for the role in order to clearly define it, so let's look a little deeper.

What is the auditor's primary task? To gather information to determine if the quality system, the procedure, the codes, whatever, are being complied with; i.e., is the company doing what it said it would do?

The auditor must understand the purpose, the scope, and the criteria for the audit. When given an assignment, auditors must ensure they understand this before they begin to plan the audit. Auditors must also understand the procedure and protocol for the audit.

The auditor must plan the audit. This usually means reviewing the criteria, studying it, analyzing it, and building a plan for the audit.

The auditor must conduct interviews. Since the auditor is an information gathering device and doesn't get any information when he or she is talking, the auditor must listen to people and observe how they perform their tasks. The auditor must also read any documentation that is available, including records of past performance—proof the company is doing what it said it would do.

To get people to communicate openly, clearly and honestly, the auditor has to use communication skills, must establish rapport, encourage communication, and ask the right kind of questions—questions that elicit detailed and honest responses.

The auditor must record the results of the audit. This means writing them down in some fashion, and they must be written in such a way that ensures understanding. The company has to take corrective action on the nonconformities found by the audit, and, therefore, must be able to understand what the auditor wrote and take action.

You can see by this brief summary that the auditor's role is a very demanding one. It is a role that taxes a lot of skills and talents, abilities and characteristics.

## Characteristics of an effective auditor

By understanding the role, we can begin to identify the characteristics an effective auditor should have. The list below is only a partial one, and you may add to your profile of an effective auditor as you build experience and insight.

- **Honesty**—the auditor must be scrupulously honest with the audited population, with his or her colleagues, and with the company. There is probably no faster or most certain way to kill an audit program than to lose the trust of the audited population. The auditor must have *integrity* and be *trustworthy*.
- **Discretion**—one way of losing the trust of the audited population is to not honor the confidentiality of observations, explanations, documents, or experiences related during an audit. External auditors, particularly those who work for registration companies, are bonded and readily sign nondisclosure agreements to ensure this discretion. Internal auditors have to carry this assurance around with them. But this discretion goes further than just the company. The auditor doesn't record names, doesn't tell people who gave him or her the information. In this regard, the auditor is like a news reporter. The auditor respects his or her sources and does not divulge their identities.
- **Knowledge**—auditors should have some knowledge in the area they are auditing. Auditors who are not knowledgeable can often be manipulated by knowledgeable auditees. Knowledge can be a two-edged sword.
- **Objectivity**—the auditor should bring a clear and independent set of eyes and mind to examining the activity. The auditor's purpose is to identify compliance and to record noncompliance. It is not the auditor's purpose to correct the process. This can be the two-edged sword of knowledge. Sometimes when an auditor is very experienced in a process or activity it is difficult for him or her to keep from saying, "Here, let me show you how we used to do it…" This trait is related to not being *opinionated* or *judgmental*.

- **Politeness**—the auditor is an invited guest in the activity, and should treat the people being audited with respect and care. This means being *tactful* and *diplomatic* with them, never being loud or crass, respecting the activity and all the protocols in the area. If the auditor exhibits an impolite manner, information will be as scarce as the fabled hen's teeth.
- **Good communication skills**—the basis of successful auditing is communication, and there are many facets to good communication.
  (1) *Establishing rapport* and *encouraging communication* is the first task of the auditor, being personable and assuring, and putting people in the right frame to answer questions honestly and completely and even to volunteer information.
  (2) Using appropriate *interviewing skills,* because the auditor needs to shape the audit, channel the experience towards the kind and type of information he or she requires. This means asking the appropriate kind of questions.
  (3) *Listening* to responses, because asking the most beautiful and probing question in the world will give you nothing if you do not listen to the answer.
  (4) Being *sensitive to* all *forms of communication,* because we receive a lot of messages through other means of communication than just what is said.
  (5) *Writing* clear, concise, and correct results, because corrective actions have to be taken for all recording nonconformities, and, often, the auditor is not around when the corrective action is taken.
- **Focus**—the auditor has a clearly-defined purpose in the audit, information to gather, and must endeavor to fulfill the scope of the audit he or she has been given. This means the auditor must stay focused on his or her

purpose. The auditor cannot be easily *distracted*, must have solid and lengthy *attention span* and good *attention to detail.*

- **Curiosity**—the successful auditor is curious about how things work, and does not accept the world as it is without trying to find out and understand more. Sometimes people without a great deal of technical knowledge can be effective as auditors because of a deep, innate sense of curiosity; they want to know—are determined to find out—how things work. Often men have a harder time at this then women do, because of a macho thing about not admitting they don't know how things work. When the car doesn't start, I'm often amused at how quickly I will open the hood and look at the infinite mystery (to me) of the modern internal combustion engine. I look at it seriously, intently, as if I could solve the problem, and, indeed, I cannot. One comic (female) noted that Moses wandered around in the wilderness looking for the promised land because even in biblical times men wouldn't stop and ask for directions! Men, don't be afraid to ask, "How does that work?" when acting as auditor.
- **Inquisitiveness**—the greatest sense of curiosity in the world won't get the auditor anywhere if he or she won't ask questions. The auditor has got to be as inquisitive as a certain, rumpled TV detective. And, like that detective, the auditor has to be:
- **Analytical**—the auditor has to analyze all the information he or she receives, pick through it, look for the diamonds in the rough, the facts, the truths that fit into the scope of the audit.
- **Thick-skinned**—the auditor cannot afford to take people's responses to him or her in a personal way. The auditor has to understand they are not reacting to him

or her. They are reacting to the situation and the idea of an *auditor*.

- **Organized**—the auditor must make the best of the time and space allocated for the audit, must be thorough—ensure he or she realizes the scope of the audit—and not waste any time. There is nothing more exasperating than to sense an auditor is lost, confused, disorganized, and is wasting time. The most effective audits are those that are carefully planned which allow for the most effective management of *time*.
- **Professional**—the auditor must make a professional impression and conduct the audit in a professional manner. You can lump a lot of things under this heading:

    (1) Being on time, and that means being neither early nor late, but being *punctual*;

    (2) Dressing and grooming appropriately, looking appropriate;

    (3) Remaining detached, not getting involved, observing from a professional distance.

I only intend this list as a partial list. As I said, you can add to the list as you build experience, and discover other characteristics that you think are important to conducting a successful audit.

The reaction to making such a list of traits is often: "There ain't nobody that good." And that is right. No one person is all these things at any given time, but we are all capable of these traits. What this exercise does is put us on notice for what is expected of us in planning, conducting and reporting on a audit. Once we understand what is expected of us, we can prepare to play that role. If you are aware of what is expected of you, then when you are given an audit assignment, you can prepare yourself to play that part.

## The Perfect Audit—and How to Achieve It

I began by noting that auditing is a fundamentally *human* activity. I use that word to underscore the fallibility of audits and auditors. In direct conflict with the subtitle above, it needs to be stated:

*There is no such thing as a perfect audit!*

All audits are imperfect, and all auditors are struggling, just like the rest of us, to achieve perfection. A clever, experienced auditor said to me some years ago, "The best audit I've ever done is the next one!" Once past a moment of laughter, I was struck by how profound this was. Auditing isn't something you can perfect, but it is something you can improve. Our goal, as auditors, is to improve with each audit. What we need is a simple self-improvement plan.

### A simple self-improvement plan

Begin by establishing a file for your self-improvement plan. Each time you complete an audit, ask and answer these three simple questions.

- What did I do that worked well during this audit?
  What was I pleased with? What went right? Did I have a good plan? Did I manage my time effectively? Did I ask good questions? Take some time to pat yourself on the back. Be specific and be honest.
- What opportunities did I miss?
  Every time you walk away from completing an audit you are going to be aware that you missed something. You'll know you didn't ask some questions you should have, that there were areas you should have looked into and didn't. There's always something. Again, be honest with yourself and write the opportunities you missed.

- What will I do differently next time I am given an audit assignment?
  Now that you know what worked for you and what you missed, you can make some decisions—while it's all fresh in your mind—about what you will do differently next time you have to do an audit. A couple of hints here: be specific. Don't write something like, "I'm gonna be better next time." This will almost guarantee that you won't be. And don't write a list of things you will do, because a list will diffuse your concentration and focus. Write down one thing that you will do differently. Write something like, "I will spend more time planning the audit," or "I will ask more open questions." Be specific and be simple.

When you have completed this self-improvement form, slip it into your file. Then, three months from now, when you are called upon to conduct an audit, you can go to the file, retrieve it and know exactly what you planned to do the next time. You don't have to sit and ponder.

## Summary

Looking at the auditor's responsibilities and activities gives a pretty clear picture of just what is required of the auditor. It's a big, demanding job. Maybe it is intimidating enough that you're looking for the exit. Don't give up. What you need are tools to help you plan, conduct, and report on the audit, and that's what we're going to help you with next.

CHAPTER 4

# Planning the Audit

## Introduction

The secret of a successful audit is in the planning. I know, I know, you've been told this about everything. "The secret to making a successful presentation is in the planning..." Well, there's a reason why you've always been told this: It's true. As with all cliches, the reason they are cliches is that they are fundamentally true.

This is especially true about auditing, and there are some very good reasons why.

- Time is the auditor's greatest enemy. The auditor always has too much to look for and not enough time to look for it. The auditor needs to use any tools he or she can to help make better use of time. Good planning is essential to managing time effectively, but you will find that time is not an enemy that is easy to defeat. Even with your best planning, you will find that time is still breathing over your shoulder. The only way you can keep time at bay is through good planning.

- The people being audited are not especially interested in the auditor accomplishing the objective of gathering information. They may have things to hide, or feel they have things to hide, and they may try to take advantage of the auditor and waste as much time as they can get away with. The only edge the auditor has is that the auditor knows what information has to be gathered and has a systematic way of making sure it is gathered.
- The auditor may be unfamiliar with the area to be audited, and may be less than confident about his or her auditing abilities. The auditor needs all the confidence he or she can muster. The better prepared the auditor is—the better plan the auditor has—the more confident they will feel. And the more in control of the audit they will be.
- There are always surprises in the area. The auditor may think he has planned all the surprises out of the audit. "I'm prepared for anything!" But once he gets there, the auditor finds unexpected things, and the unexpected things are not irrelevant. They are important. Good planning allows the auditor to take advantage of the unexpected, not be a victim of it.

## Preplanning Preparation

There are a few things auditors should know even before they can begin to plan. There's information they need, and questions they need answers to in order to plan the audit. For example, before they begin any audit, auditors should be familiar with the procedure governing their actions as auditors. If they are internal auditors, then they need to read and be familiar with the internal audit procedure; if they are auditing a supplier, then they need to be aware of the procedure governing the evaluation of subcontractors.

## Receiving the audit assignment

Someone is going to assign the auditor to conduct the audit. This may be the manager of the internal audit program, or it may be a client who is hiring the auditor to conduct an audit, or it may be a quality manager who needs the auditor to conduct an audit on a suppler. Someone is going to give the auditor the assignment. In the initial briefing, here are some of the things the auditor should be told, and if the auditor is not told these things, he or she should ask the questions.

- The *subject* of the audit.
  Who is being audited? What department or activity is supposed to be audited?
- The *date* and *place* for the audit.
  Auditors need to know where they are supposed to be and when they are supposed to be there. In some systems the auditor may not be given an exact date and time, depending upon the procedure. Auditors may be given a deadline, or a window within which they are responsible for setting the exact date and time. This is discussed later in the section on preaudit activities. The auditor should be given either an exact date and time or a window of time.
- The *purpose* of the audit.
  Why is this audit being conducted? What are the objectives? What is it to achieve? In the case of a normally scheduled internal audit, that may be the entire purpose: "This is a regularly scheduled internal audit." This may be purpose enough, but there may be other purposes for the audit. There may be a customer audit scheduled next week, and this is a readiness audit, to

see how how ready a department or activity is. There may have been a customer audit a week ago, and this is a follow-up audit to check on the progress of corrective action. This may be a follow-up audit to "...ensure corrective action has been taken and is effective."

- The *scope* of the audit.
  How deep a look is the auditor supposed to take? How wide a look? Sometimes auditors may be asked to audit only a small part of an activity or a procedure, and they may be asked to take a narrow, deep view. Other times, the auditor may be asked to plan an audit over an entire process or procedure, and the scope may be shallow but wide. The scope of the audit gives the auditor the boundaries they are supposed to work within.
- The *criteria* for the audit.
  These are the planned arrangements to which the audit subjects are going to be audited against, the system to which they should be complying. The auditor should either be given a set of the criteria or be told what the criteria are so that he or she can get a set.
- Any *special information* about the activity to be audited.
  At any given time, in any given area, there can be relationships, situations, perhaps an atmosphere, which the auditor needs to be warned of or at least alerted to. These are things that if not known could impact on the effectiveness of the audit. Auditors have an objective and precious time to achieve it, and must be aware of anything that could keep them from accomplishing their objective.

## Preaudit activities

With the audit assignment in hand, the auditor probably needs more information before setting and planning the audit. There may be a need to visit the activity to be audited or at least have some communication with the responsible people.

### Second- or third-party audits

Second- or third-party auditors may be strangers to the organization or activity they are auditing. If this is the case, there is a lot the auditor needs to know. Often with a third-party audit there is too much money and valuable time involved for the auditor (or team leader) to visit the organization, so he or she gets the information by using questionnaires or by telephone. Second-party auditors may have more freedom and may get this information in person. In order to plan the audit the auditor might want to know:

- The exact location of the organization or activity.
  Where is the organization located? What are the directions to the organization's facility? How far is the organization from the airport? Are there hotels nearby? How far is the organization from hotels? If the team leader can't get this information by visiting the organization in person, he or she may use a map.
- The physical size of the organization or activity.
  How many buildings are in the facility? How many square feet? Are the buildings close together or separated? How long will it take to get from one department to another? If the team leader can't get this information in person, he or she may request a facilities layout drawing.
- The number of employees.
  How many people? How many shifts? How is the workforce organized? How many administrative? Production? Marketing? Design? and so on.
- The number of processes.
  How many processes are included within the scope of this audit?
- The complexity of processes.
  How complicated are the processes that are included in the scope of this audit.

- More of the documented system (if appropriate).
  After conducting a document review (adequacy audit) of the quality manual, the team leader may request other documentation to aid in the planning.
- Organization structure.
  How is the organization structured? Is there an up-to-date organization chart?
- Results of previous audits.
  If this information is available it is invaluable in planning. It may not be available during the planning stage, and the audit team may not see it until they are on-site.
- Any certificates the organization might have.
  Does this organization carry any regulatory certificates or customer certificates, such as Boeing D-9000?
- How it views its own performance.
- Logistics.
  In addition to information about the company, the team leader needs to find out information about the company's location and external facilities. What's the closest airport? How far is the company from the airport? What is the closest hotel or motel? Can he or she have luncheons catered in for the team? Can the team have an exclusive table in the company lunch room?
- Anything else that will aid in the planning.
  In addition to finding out how many employees there are, the team leader will want to know what is the predominant language spoken at the site. Is there a union? The team leader will want to know who the union leadership is. Are there any special safety or educational requirements? If the audit is being conducted at a chemical plant, there is an educational requirement. The time for the safety briefing must be figured into the plan. Is there any special equipment that is required?

In short, anything that is important to conducting this audit successfully.

### Internal audits

Some internal audit programs are very simple and clear-cut. The auditor is given the assignment and in the assignment is a specific time and place for the audit. The auditor shows up, conducts the audit and reports on the findings and that's it.

Recently, there has been some movement to give the internal auditor a little more freedom in this process.

Some systems now require the internal auditor to visit the activity to be audited for planning purposes before the audit. If a visit is not logistically possible—the sites are some miles apart, for example—the objective of the preaudit visit can be accomplished over the telephone.

During the preaudit visit, the following are done:

- An exact date and time for the audit can be established. If the auditor has been given an envelope, say three days or a week, an exact time for the audit—within that envelope—can be agreed upon. This makes the audit subject part of the process, and allows for flexibility in the scheduling of the audit.
- The purpose and scope for the audit is presented.
- The criteria to be used is agreed upon.
  Auditors must make sure they are auditing the activity to the same documentation they are working to.
- An internal schedule for the audit can be drawn up and agreed to.
  Once an exact time for the audit is worked out, the auditor and the audit subject may work out a detailed schedule. The auditor may want to see the manager for a half-hour, then the supervisor, and so forth.
- Availability of essential people is ensured.
- Any special information about the activity is noted.

As important as these activities are, something even more important can happen during this preaudit visit that can have a big impact on the conduct of the audit. During this preaudit visit a rapport is established between the auditor and the people within the activity. They get to know each other. When the actual audit begins, very little time needs to be spent in doing this. It has already been done. Thus, some time can be saved.

There are probably a few voices left out there crying for the "surprise audit." These people want the auditor to catch people doing things wrong and they firmly believe the audit won't catch them if they are warned it is coming. "Why, they clean up their act and you won't find anything wrong!" Personally, I don't care. If they clean up their act and comply with their system, that's fine. They very likely won't be able to hide past noncompliance because they won't change records, so there will be evidence to find.

Most organizations these days eschew the surprise audit. There is very little value in it, and there can be great danger in it. The danger is that it builds resentment and distrust in the audited population. I think I said this before: if there is one sure way to kill an audit program, it is through the loss of trust in the audited population.

There are fewer and fewer surprise audits conducted, and, hopefully, there won't be any in the future.

Once the auditor has a clear picture of the organization or activity to be audited, they can begin to plan the audit.

## Planning the Audit

Depending upon the type of audit that is to be conducted, the first activity may be a review of the documented system. Remember this type of audit is often called an adequacy audit or, simply, a document review. The purpose of such an audit is to determine if a documented system meets the requirements of the applicable standard—is it adequate? In the case of third-party audit, whether or not the compliance portion of the assessment is conducted at all depends upon the success of the document review. If the documented system does not meet the requirements of the applicable standard, the compliance audit may be postponed.

Internal auditors usually do not conduct these types of audits. The internal auditor is usually auditing an operating system. This does not mean the internal auditor won't be doing document reviews. They may. If a system has not been audited against any outside criteria, a document review may be used as an internal audit. Also, the internal auditor may run into new procedures that have not been compared to the outside standard or code. So it is possible internal auditors will find themselves conducting adequacy audits.

## Planning the document review (adequacy audit)

Remember the purpose of this audit is ensure the documented system meets the requirement of the applicable criteria, which may be a standard, regulation, or a code. I am going to use ISO 9001/2 as the outside document, but the steps will work with any document.

- Get a copy of the applicable criteria.
  This may be ISO 9001, ISO 9002, or other standard or code or regulation. It is whatever set of criteria the documented system was created to meet.
- Review the requirements.
  Read the criteria carefully. Read them for the *intent* of the requirements. In the case of the ISO 9001/2 standard there is a common fault of reading too much into the words, for example:

  The 1994 version of ISO 9001/2, under "Document Control," states:

> *"A master list or equivalent document control procedure shall be established to identify the current revision of documents and be readily available to preclude the use of invalid and/or obsolete documents."*

The intent of this requirement is that there be some method to identify the current revision of the quality system documents. The intent is *not* that there should be a master list. So in identifying the requirement the auditor would look to see that the system has some method of identifying the current revision of documents.

- Record the *intent* of the requirements.

Once the auditor has identified the requirements, he or she can record them. There should be at least one notation for every requirement of the applicable standard. In ISO 9001, that means there are at least 20, and in ISO 9002, there are at least 19. Truthfully, though, for most of the requirements there will be more than one notation, as shown in Table 4–1.

**Table 4–1** Requirements

| ISO 9001/2 Paragraph | Requirement |
|---|---|
| 4.1 Management Responsibility | 1. Is there a documented quality policy?<br>2. Is responsibility, authority and interrelation defined and documented?<br>3. Are resource requirements identified?<br>4. Has a management representative been appointed?<br>5. Are management reviews required at defined intervals?<br>6. Are records kept of management reviews? |

These six questions, or points, all come out of the first paragraph of 9001/2. These things should be found in the documented system.

There will be some requirements in the document that the auditor will not be able to find out about from a document review. For example, ISO 9001/2 requires that the quality policy must be "*...understood, implemented and maintained at all levels in the organization.*" The auditor can't learn this from a review of the documents. The auditor must go to the facility and ask the employees about their understanding of quality policy, what it means to them and their job, and so forth.

When the intent of the requirements has been identified and documented, the auditor is ready to get the system documents for examination and comparison. We'll talk about conducting a document review later in another chapter of this book.

## A matrix of a system

From identifying what is required for each paragraph of the applicable standard, the auditor can build a matrix for the system. This is a valuable tool and can serve as a record of the document review as well as a planning document for the compliance audit.

A version of a complete matrix for a documented system is included at the end of this chapter. Only a portion is shown in Figure 4–1. The sample matrix is done to ISO 9001, but the same principles can be be applied to any standard. Simply put, such a matrix may include:

- The paragraph number and title from the applicable standard
- The requirements for each paragraph
- A policy reference—where the requirement is addressed in policy
- A procedure reference—where the requirement is addressed by procedure

- A comments section for any notes the auditor wishes to make

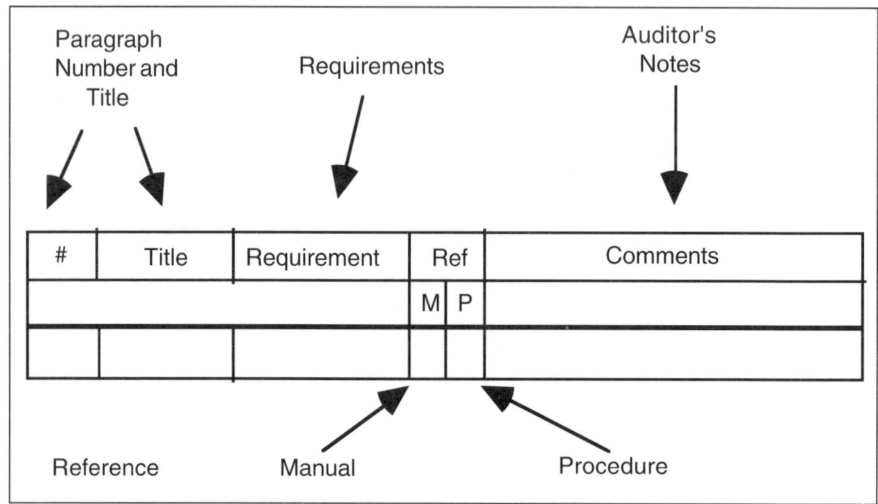


**Figure 4–1** Document matrix

This sample matrix has an additional column for recording nonconformities. This is not a requirement for a document matrix, but it might be helpful to keep track of problems.

In the next chapter we will discuss completing the document matrix as we conduct an adequacy audit.

## Planning the Compliance Audit

Remember the purpose of this type of audit is to ensure that the organization or activity is complying—using, working to—the documented system.

The document review told the auditor that the documented system met the requirements of the applicable standard. The system is a good system. Next, the compliance audit is scheduled, and this audit will tell the auditor that this good system has been implemented.

## Reviewing the criteria

Once the auditor has received the assignment, the planning becomes more personal. If the audit is to be conducted to the documented quality system, which is true in most cases, then the auditor builds the plan on those procedures. If there is no documented system, or if the auditor cannot obtain the documented system, then the auditor may use the standard as a planning document.

If the standard is used as the planning document, the auditor may build a plan based on the requirements of the standard. If the auditor did a document review, then they are familiar with the requirements of the standard. We will discuss building a generic checklist later in this section.

The auditor may be building the audit on the documented system, procedures, and instructions. The procedures and instructions to be audited may not be familiar to the auditor. The auditor needs to review the criteria and become familiar with the contents. Since the auditor is looking for compliance to procedures, the auditor does not necessarily have to be an expert in the area they are auditing. They need to understand the process well enough to ask the right questions. This understanding begins with a review of the criteria in a systematic manner.

- *Read* the procedures carefully.
  Initially, just try to understand the process. Don't try to analyze the process at first, just read it.
- Try to understand the *flow* of the activity.
  Try to understand what happens and when it happens, look for relationships within the process.

- Identify the *key players* and what they do in the process. Start a list of key players, and identify the hand-off points.
- Identify the *inputs* and the *outputs* of the steps in the process.
  What starts the process? Do the steps in the process produce something? What is it?

An example of such an document analysis is shown in Table 4–2.

**Table 4–2** Document analysis

| Procedure | Analysis |
|---|---|
| 4.2 Process | |
| Production Control provides the Department Supervisor with a weekly Production Schedule (form 226). | Input: Production Schedule |
| The Department Supervisor draws up the work order for the job, including tasks and specifications on form 879. | Personnel<br>• Production Control<br>• Department Supervisor<br>• Inventory<br>• Employee(s) |
| The Department Supervisor makes up a Parts Request (form 475) and takes it to Inventory. | |
| Inventory draws the necessary parts and completes the Parts Request. The parts and the form are delivered to the Department Supervisor. The completed Parts Request is filed in the Department Supervisor's office. | Forms:<br>• Production Schedule, form 226<br>• Work order, form 879<br>• Parts Request, form 475<br>• Employee Loading Record, form 364 |
| The Department Supervisor completes the Employee Loading Record (form 364) and assigns jobs and parts to employees. | Output: finished product, boxed, in inventory. |
| Parts are completed as per work order. Finished product is boxed and sent to Inventory. | |

Flow-charting skills can come in very handy here in understanding a process. Sometimes roughing out a chart of the process flow will help the auditor understand it.

## Preparing the audit plan

As auditors analyze the process they note the steps in the process, the key players, and the inputs/outputs. This information will become the basis of the audit plan.

The most commonly used term for an audit plan is checklist. Most everyone calls audit plans, checklists. I try to avoid using the word checklist for the audit plan. My reasoning is simple. "Checklist" connotes a set of structured "yes/no" questions, as shown in Table 4–3.

**Table 4-3** Traditional checklist

| # | Question | Yes | No |
|---|---|---|---|
| 1. | Do you have a procedure for document control? | | |
| 2. | Is your procedure for document control followed in the department? | | |

This type of checklist is very simple to use. The question is read and the answer is checked off. We have probably all been audited with this kind of checklist. The last one I ran across was developed in the chemical business to audit compliance with product identification and safety regulations. It was constructed in just this fashion.

It doesn't take very long to see that this type of checklist—used in that fashion—doesn't get the kind of information the auditor is looking for on quality audits. The auditor can come back with a completed checklist of hundreds of questions and not have any real understanding of what is going on in the activity.

In defense of this type of checklist, they are often not intended to be used as a list of questions to ask the person being audited. Their intention is to provide the auditor with a guide. The auditor was supposed to use the sample questions as guides for conducting the audit. Human nature being what it is, it is so much easier to just fall back to using the questions and checking off the answers. This is particularly true of neophyte auditors who might be a little intimidated at the process altogether.

Oh, give me a crutch and I will surely use it.

I am going to suggest to you a different format. I believe you will find this different format much more beneficial in conducting the audit. I also believe you will find it a better tool for getting the depth of information you need. I call this document the "audit plan," but you may call it whatever you want. The questions written on the plan or checklist give structure to the audit and are a plan to follow. It is all worked out ahead of the actual audit itself. It guarantees the scope of the audit will be covered and that time will be used most effectively.

In team audits, the audit plan is done is two stages. The team leader plans the entire audit, deciding which auditor goes where and when, and creates the overall plan, schedule and structure for the audit. This overall audit plan may take many different forms. One such form is shown in Table 4–4.

**Table 4–4** Audit plan

| Personnel | Day 1 | Day 2 | Day 3 |
|---|---|---|---|
| Team Lead | • Mgt. Rev<br>• Int. audit<br>• Qual. Sys. | • Records<br>• Cor/Pre<br>• Stat. Tech. | • Train.<br>• Control of Non-Con. Product |
| Auditor #1 | • Contract Review<br>• Doc. Control | • Purch.<br>• Warehouse | • Cust. Supplied Product<br>• Servicing |
| Auditor #2 | • Design Control | • Design<br>• Inspection and Test | • Process Control |

Table 4–4 is an example of what an audit plan may look like for a three person/three day audit (nine person-days). Where each auditor on the team will be is given. The shaded areas depict those events where everyone is involved. The first shaded column represents the opening meeting, the next two daily "wrap up" meetings and the last, the closing meeting.

Once the overall plan has been made up, and the auditors' assignments given, then each of the auditors plans their part of the audit.

Most internal audits are conducted on an individual basis, and the auditor does all the work himself.

### Generic audit plans

If auditors do not have access to the specific procedures they are going to be auditing people to, then they may begin by building a generic audit plan with the applicable standard. They will review the standard and select the audit points from it. They will begin the audit plan in this fashion (Table 4–5).

In this fashion, the auditor can begin to build a generic audit plan for each part of the system. The key points may be

**Table 4–5** Key points and standard requirement

| Standard Requirement | Key Point |
|---|---|
| 4.18 Training | |
| The supplier shall establish and maintain documented procedures for identifying training needs and provide for the training of all personnel performing activities affecting quality. Personnel performing specific assigned tasks shall be qualified on the basis of appropriate education, training, and/or experience, as required. Appropriate records of training shall be maintained (see 4.16).. | • Documented procedures<br>• Procedures for identifying the training needs<br>• Providing the training<br>• Other qualifications<br>• Records |

translated into audit points as is described in the section on specific audit plans.

### Specific audit plans

Specific audit plans are built to the documented procedures.

The auditor begins by reviewing the documents he or she is going to audit to, as was mentioned earlier. These may be policies, procedures, or instructions. As the auditor reads the documents, he or she looks for points at which they should be able to see something being performed or get something in their hand. These points are "audit points." An example is shown in Table 4–6.

**Table 4–6** Audit points

| Procedure | Audit Point |
|---|---|
| The Purchase Office keeps the pink copy of the purchase order. | • Pink copy of purchase order |
| Purchase orders are filed alphabetically by vendor name. | • Filed alphabetically by vendor name |

There are some common threads through all systems that are designed to meet the ISO 9000 standards. These common threads are a good foundation for the audit plan. For example, the standard requires that everyone understand the quality policy. That may be the first point on the audit plan. Another example of a common thread is corrective action taken from previous audits. This is another good place to start.

Keep track of the audit points. These form the audit plan. As was said earlier, this may take different forms. For example:

- Some auditors write the points up in the form of questions, as:

*"Is there a pink copy of the purchase order?*
*"Are the purchase orders filed alphabetically?"*

- Others write the points up in a directive (imperative) format, as:

  *"Ask for pink copy of purchase order."*
  *"See if purchase orders are filed alphabetically."*

- Others mark up a copy of the procedure, as:

  *"The Purchase Office keeps and files the* pink copy *of the Purchase Order in* Alphabetical order."

### Some sample audit plan formats

As we said, the audit plan may take many formats, or have no format at all—a marked up procedure, for example. The auditor, particularly an internal auditor, may have no choice, he or she may be given a pre-printed format and be asked to use it. It doesn't matter what shape or form the audit plan takes, they generally have:

- A space for the audit point; and
- A space for notes or comments.

In its simplest form, the audit plan might look like Figure 4–2:

| Audit Point | Comment |
|---|---|
| 1. Ask for pink copy of p.o. | |
| 2. See p.o.'s filed alphabetically by vendor name | |
| Etc. | |

**Figure 4–2** Audit plan

This is the simplest format the audit plan might take. There is a column for the auditor to write in the audit point, and the other column is for any notes the auditor might take about the results. Sometimes this format—or any of the formats—is "landscaped," turned 90 degrees, which allows for less audit points per page but more room for making notes.

| Audit Point | Comments | Time |
|---|---|---|
| 1. Ask for pink copy of p.o. | | |
| 2. See p.o.'s filed alphabetically by vendor name | | |
| Etc. | | |

**Figure 4–3** Audit plan

In Figure 4–3, a third column—for time—is added. A time column like this can be helpful in time management during the audit. For example, if there is an hour allocated for the audit and ten audit points, that is six minutes per audit point. The auditor can use this column to keep track of how much time is spent on each audit point.

| Audit Point | Observation | Nonconformance | Comment |
|---|---|---|---|
| 1. Ask for pink copy of p.o. | | | |
| 2. See p.o.'s filed alphabetically by vendor name | | | |
| Etc. | | | |

**Figure 4–4** Audit plan

In Figure 4–4, two additional columns have been added. The "Observation" column is for the auditor to note what was actually found or observed. The "Nonconformance" column is for the auditor to write what the observation was a nonconformance against, if any, and the "comment" section is for any additional notes the auditor might wish to make.

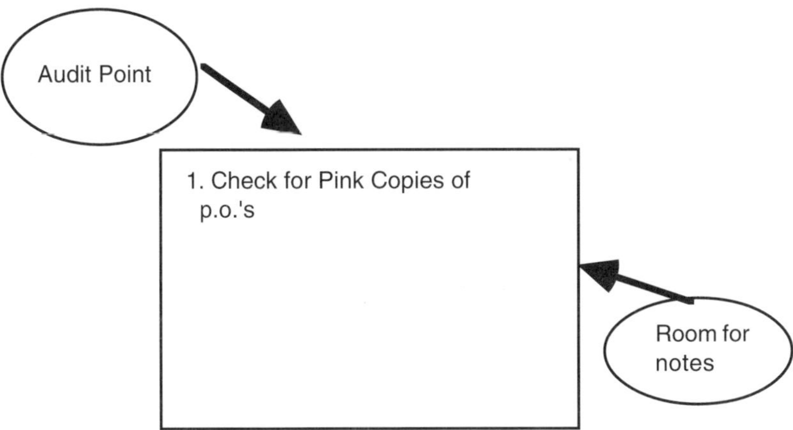


**Figure 4–5** 3 × 5 index card

My own personal choice is 3 × 5 index cards, Figure 4–5. These are available most anywhere. Use one card for each audit point and assemble them in the order you want to follow. You make your audit point on the top of the card and leave the rest for your notes. When you have covered this audit point, you can slip the card to the back of the stack, and your next audit point appears.

One aspect of the index cards that I like personally is that you can come to the audit with your hands free. A lot of auditors like to use clipboards, and they are a helpful device. The other types of forms we have looked at lend themselves to clipboards. I don't like clipboards. I like to make my audit plan up on index cards and put the cards in my pocket.

Another method of creating a working document is to mark up the procedure you are auditing to. Simply make a copy of the procedure and take a pen or pencil—red is preferred—and highlight the audit points within the procedure. A sample is shown in Figure 4–6.

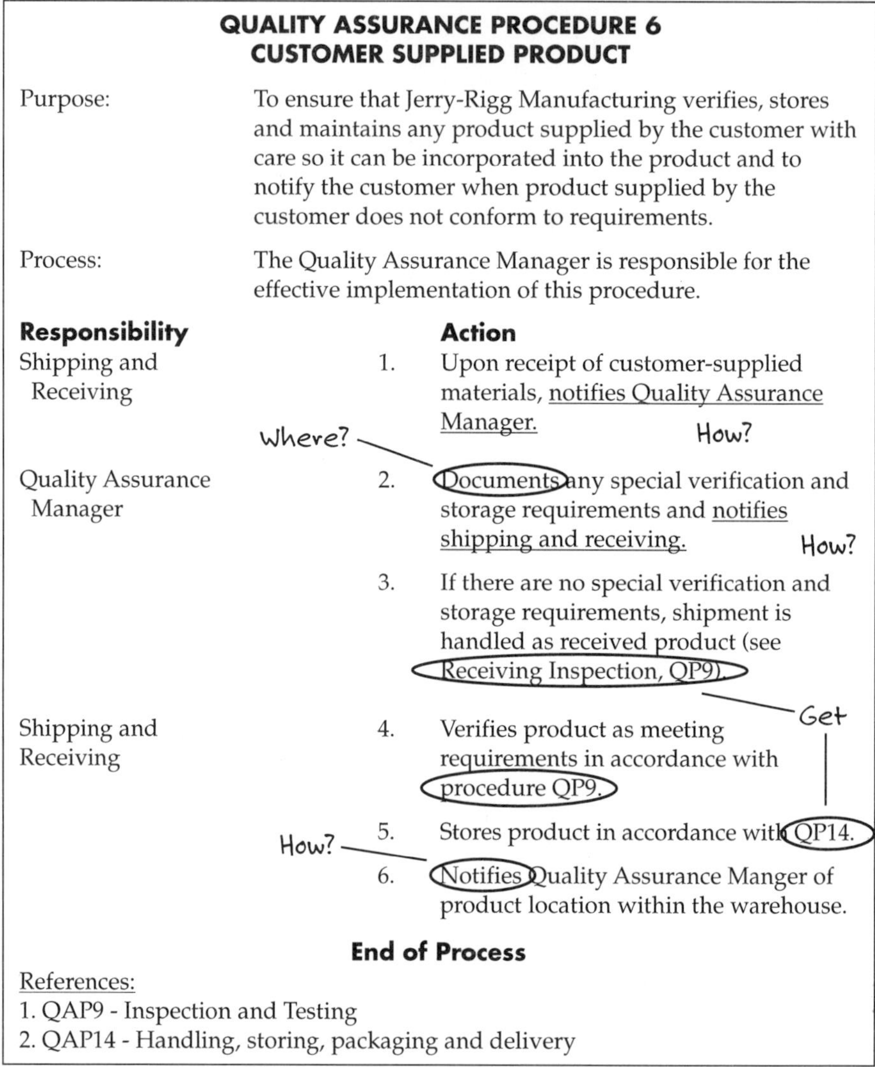

**QUALITY ASSURANCE PROCEDURE 6**
**CUSTOMER SUPPLIED PRODUCT**

Purpose: To ensure that Jerry-Rigg Manufacturing verifies, stores and maintains any product supplied by the customer with care so it can be incorporated into the product and to notify the customer when product supplied by the customer does not conform to requirements.

Process: The Quality Assurance Manager is responsible for the effective implementation of this procedure.

| **Responsibility** | | **Action** |
|---|---|---|
| Shipping and Receiving | 1. | Upon receipt of customer-supplied materials, notifies Quality Assurance Manager. |
| Quality Assurance Manager | 2. | Documents any special verification and storage requirements and notifies shipping and receiving. |
| | 3. | If there are no special verification and storage requirements, shipment is handled as received product (see Receiving Inspection, QP9). |
| Shipping and Receiving | 4. | Verifies product as meeting requirements in accordance with procedure QP9. |
| | 5. | Stores product in accordance with QP14. |
| | 6. | Notifies Quality Assurance Manger of product location within the warehouse. |

**End of Process**

References:
1. QAP9 - Inspection and Testing
2. QAP14 - Handling, storing, packaging and delivery



**Figure 4–6** Marked up procedure

This makes the audit points clearly visible and gives the auditor the minimum number of pieces of paper to carry around. The major drawback of this method is that it provides little or no space for note-taking.

## Summary

It should be clear by now that whatever form it takes, the audit plan has a lot of uses.

- Helps you manage your time effectively.
- Provides a means of note-taking.
- Becomes a part of the record of the audit.
- Is a means to "speak" with other auditors.

| Para # | Paragraph Title | Requirements | Reference | | Comments | NC |
|---|---|---|---|---|---|---|
| | | | Man | Pro | | |
| 4.1 | Management responsibility | | | | | |
| 4.1.1 | Quality policy | Documented quality policy<br>Must be understood, implemented, and maintained | | | | |
| 4.1.2 | Organization | | | | | |
| 4.1.2.1 | Authority and responsibility | Define and document authority and responsibility | | | | |
| 4.1.2.2 | Resources | Identify resource requirements | | | | |
| 4.1.2.3 | Management representative | Appoint management representative | | | | |
| 4.1.3 | Management review | Conduct management review at defined intervals<br>Keep records | | | | |
| 4.2 | Quality system | | | | | |
| 4.2.1 | General | Must have documented system<br>Must have a quality manual<br>Quality manual must contain or reference procedures | | | | |
| 4.2.2 | Quality system procedures | Must have documented procedures<br>Must be effectively implemented | | | | |
| 4.2.3 | Quality planning | Document how requirements for quality will be met | | | | |

**An Adequacy Audit Matrix for ISO 9001**

| Para # | Paragraph Title | Requirements | Reference | | Comments | NC |
|---|---|---|---|---|---|---|
| | | | Man | Pro | | |
| 4.3 | Contract review | | | | | |
| 4.3.1 | General | Documented procedures | | | | |
| 4.3.2 | Review | Each contract reviewed | | | | |
| 4.3.3 | Amendment to contract | Identify how amendment to contract is made and transferred | | | | |
| 4.3.4 | Records | Records of contract review are maintained | | | | |
| 4.4 | Design control | | | | | |
| 4.4.1 | General | Documented procedures to control and verify the design | | | | |
| 4.4.2 | Design and development planning | Prepare plans for each design and development activity | | | | |
| 4.4.3 | Organizational and technical interfaces | Defined<br>Necessary information documented, transmitted, and reviewed | | | | |
| 4.4.4 | Design input | Documented<br>Reviewed for adequacy | | | | |
| 4.4.5 | Design output | Documented<br>Expressed in terms that can be verified and validated<br>Reviewed before release | | | | |
| 4.4.6 | Design review | Documented<br>Planned and conducted at appropriate stages<br>Included representatives<br>Records | | | | |

**An Adequacy Audit Matrix for ISO 9001 (continued)**

| Para # | Paragraph Title | Requirements | Reference | | Comments | NC |
|---|---|---|---|---|---|---|
| | | | Man | Pro | | |
| 4.4.7 | Design verification | Conducted<br>Measures recorded | | | | |
| 4.4.8 | Design validation | Performed | | | | |
| 4.4.9 | Design changes | Documented<br>Reviewed and approved | | | | |
| 4.5 | Document and data control | | | | | |
| 4.5.1 | General | Documented procedures | | | | |
| 4.5.2 | Document and data approval and issue | Documents reviewed and approved<br>A master list or equivalent<br>Pertinent issues available<br>Invalid/obsolete documents removed or identified | | | | |
| 4.5.3 | Document and data changes | Reviewed and approved<br>(Where appropriate) nature of change identified | | | | |
| 4.6 | Purchasing | | | | | |
| 4.6.1 | General | Documented procedures | | | | |
| 4.6.2 | Evaluation of subcontractors | On their ability to meet requirements<br>Define type and extent of control<br>Establish and maintain records of acceptable subcontractors | | | | |

**An Adequacy Audit Matrix for ISO 9001 (continued)**

| Para # | Paragraph Title | Requirements | Reference | | Comments | NC |
|---|---|---|---|---|---|---|
| | | | Man | Pro | | |
| 4.6.3 | Purchasing data | Purchasing documents clearly describe product<br>Reviewed and approved prior to release | | | | |
| 4.6.4 | Verification of purchased product | | | | | |
| 4.6.4.1 | Supplier verification at subcontractor's premises | Specify arrangements in purchasing documents | | | | |
| 4.6.4.2 | Customer verification of subcontracted product | (Where specified in contract) afforded the right to conduct | | | | |
| 4.7 | Control of customer-supplied product | Documented procedures | | | | |
| 4.8 | Product identification and traceability | (Where appropriate) documented procedures<br>(Where traceability is a requirement) document procedures<br>Records of identification | | | | |
| 4.9 | Process control | Identify, plan processes<br>Ensure processes are controlled, to include:<br>documented procedures (work instructions)<br>suitable equipment<br>suitable environment<br>compliance<br>approval of equipment and processes<br>criteria for workmanship<br>maintenance | | | | |

**An Adequacy Audit Matrix for ISO 9001 (continued)**

| Para # | Paragraph Title | Requirements | Reference | | Comments | NC |
|---|---|---|---|---|---|---|
| | | | Man | Pro | | |
| 4.10 | Inspection and testing | | | | | |
| 4.10.1 | General | Documented procedures | | | | |
| 4.10.2 | Receiving inspection and testing | | | | | |
| 4.10.2.1 | | Ensure only verified product is used | | | | |
| 4.10.2.2 | | Related to subcontractor evaluation (see 4.6) | | | | |
| 4.10.2.3 | | Unverified product released for urgent production purposes identified and recorded | | | | |
| 4.10.3 | In-process inspection and testing | Documented procedures<br>Identify unverified product released for urgent production purposes | | | | |
| 4.10.4 | Final inspection and testing | Documented procedures<br>Specify all inspections and tests have been carried out | | | | |
| 4.10.5 | Inspection and test records | To provide evidence that inspections/tests have been carried out<br>To identify authority for release | | | | |
| 4.11 | Control of inspection, measuring, and test equipment | | | | | |

**An Adequacy Audit Matrix for ISO 9001 (continued)**

| Para # | Paragraph Title | Requirements | Reference | | Comments | NC |
|---|---|---|---|---|---|---|
| | | | Man | Pro | | |
| 4.11.1 | General | Documented procedures<br>Check/recheck devices<br>Provide measurement data when requested | | | | |
| 4.11.2 | Control procedure | Determine measurement<br>Accuracy<br>Select appropriate equipment<br>Identify equipment<br>State basis for calibration<br>Define process<br>Maintain records<br>Environment conditions<br>Handling<br>Protect equipment | | | | |
| 4.12 | Inspection and test status | Documented procedures | | | | |
| 4.13 | Control of nonconforming product | | | | | |
| 4.13.1 | General | Documented procedures providing for the<br>identification<br>documentation<br>evaluation<br>segregation<br>disposition<br>notification | | | | |
| 4.13.2 | Review and disposition of nonconforming product | Define responsibility for review and authority to disposition<br>Reinspect after rework/repair according to procedures | | | | |
| 4.14 | Corrective and preventive action | | | | | |

**An Adequacy Audit Matrix for ISO 9001 (continued)**

| Para # | Paragraph Title | Requirements | Reference Man | Reference Pro | Comments | NC |
|---|---|---|---|---|---|---|
| 4.14.1 | General | Documented procedures<br>Implement and record any changes to procedures | | | | |
| 4.14.2 | Corrective action | Procedures shall include:<br>effective handling of customer complaints<br>investigation of causes<br>determination of corrective action<br>application of controls | | | | |
| 4.14.3 | Preventive action | Procedures shall include<br>use of information<br>determination of steps<br>initiation of preventive action<br>information to management review | | | | |
| 4.15 | Handling, storage, packaging, preservation, and delivery | | | | | |
| 4.15.1 | General | Documented procedures | | | | |
| 4.15.2 | Handling | Methods to prevent damage or deterioration | | | | |
| 4.15.3 | Storage | Designated storage areas<br>Methods for receipt and dispatch<br>Reassessment | | | | |
| 4.15.4 | Packaging | Control processes and materials | | | | |
| 4.15.5 | Preservation | Methods for preservation and segregation | | | | |

**An Adequacy Audit Matrix for ISO 9001 (continued)**

| Para # | Paragraph Title | Requirements | Reference | | Comments | NC |
|---|---|---|---|---|---|---|
| | | | Man | Pro | | |
| 4.15.6 | Delivery | Protect the product after final inspection | | | | |
| 4.16 | Control of quality records | Documented procedures for the: identification collection indexing accessing filing storage maintenance disposition of quality records Retention times established and recorded | | | | |
| 4.17 | Internal quality audits | Documented procedures Scheduled Record results Bring results to attention of responsible personnel Follow-up activities | | | | |
| 4.18 | Training | Documented procedures Records | | | | |
| 4.19 | Servicing | Documented procedures | | | | |
| 4.20 | Statistical techniques | | | | | |
| 4.20.1 | Identification of need | Identify the need for statistical techniques | | | | |
| 4.20.2 | Procedures | Documented procedures to implement and control | | | | |

**An Adequacy Audit Matrix for ISO 9001 (continued)**

# CHAPTER 5

# Conducting the Adequacy Audit

## Introduction

Remember, an adequacy audit—document review—is a comparison of a documented quality system to the applicable standard. This may be ISO 9001/2, which is what I am using in this book, or it may be any regulation or other standard or code.

In the last chapter, I discussed how to prepare the adequacy audit by reviewing the applicable standard, capturing the intent of the requirements. I suggested the auditor build an audit plan for this audit by identifying the requirements of the applicable standard. I called this audit plan an adequacy audit matrix.

In this section, we're going to look at conducting the adequacy audit according to this plan.

## Elements of the Adequacy Audit

Ah, let's go back to the very beginning. Remember the three elements of an audit are:

- gathering information;
- comparing the information to known criteria; and
- if there's a gap, finding out why.

Let's apply these elements to the adequacy audit.

### Gathering information

The review of the documented quality system may be limited to only the top or policy-level documents, if the system is put together that way. So the auditor may have only the policy manual to review. This may be sufficient, depending upon how well the policy manual was conceived and written. Policy manuals often give a good, clear picture of the system, describing its scope and application, its parts, and how the parts fit together. Sometimes the policy manual will provide the auditor with a cross-reference of the other parts of the system, a "skeleton key" into the system.

If the system was not developed in levels and has only one level, the auditor will have access to the entire system at one setting.

If the auditor only has the policy-level documents and this proves to be insufficient, the auditor may contact the organization and ask for other parts of the system documents.

The auditor gathers information during the adequacy audit, primarily, by reading. The parts of the documented system available to the auditor are read. This is why this type of audit is sometimes known as a desk-top audit, because it normally only involves the auditor, in the privacy of his or her own surroundings, reading the system.

Some interviewing skills might be called upon. For example, if the auditor feels that the portion of the system available is not sufficient, he or she may call and request additional parts of the system.

Also, the auditor may have to call the organization for any clarification required. During the audit, the auditor may find ambiguities or contradictions. The auditor calls and asks for clarification.

## Comparing

Obviously, the document system is being compared to the applicable standard.

The comparison is made requirement by requirement, section by section. The audit plan has the intent of each requirement. The auditor reads the applicable portion in the documented system and ensures that it meets the intent of the requirement. If it does not, there is a nonconformance and a nonconformance report is written (see Chapter 7, Reporting on the Audit).

If the auditor does not understand something in the system, the auditor calls or talks to the person responsible for the document to get clarification.

If the adequacy audit is being conducted over an entire system, the auditor looks for complete coverage of the requirements of the applicable standard. Nothing can be skipped. If a section of the standard does not apply to an organization, the documented system must tell the auditor this. Any blanks—holes—are nonconformances.

**The documented system must address every requirement of the applicable standard.**

### Finding out why

This particular element of an audit is not as critical on the adequacy audit as on the compliance audit. But the question should be asked. A nonconformance may have occurred because of an omission or a misunderstanding. The auditor can ask the questions and it may help the company in correcting the situation.

## Understanding the System

Before reviewing the details of the system, the auditor should try to get a grasp on the whole system. I always begin a document review by turning to the section of the manual I'm reviewing that addresses the structure of the quality system. In some systems this section correlates with paragraph 4.2 of the standard, and is entitled "Section 2" or something similar. I go through this section to get a picture of the documented system. I take this direction from Paragraph (requirement, element) 4.2 of the standard, which is shown in Table 5–1.

Reading this section of the manual should give the auditor an idea of the documented system. In truth, the auditor has no idea what they are going to find. The standard itself does not define the quality system any further than this. It goes on to talk about the procedures that form a part of the system and there's a section on quality planning, but there is nothing that describes what a quality system should look like. So companies are free to design and build their own documented systems according to:

- the demands of the business;
- the requirements of the customers; and
- any regulatory requirements.

Because of this freedom, the auditor is not really sure when they begin to review a system exactly what they are going to find. However, the auditor should find a portion of the quality manual that describes the system.

**Table 5–1** Quality manual requirement

| Standard Requirement | Key Points |
|---|---|
| 4.2 Quality system | |
| 4.2.1 General | |
| The supplier shall establish, document and maintain a quality system as a means of ensuring that product conforms to specified requirements. The supplier shall prepare a quality manual covering the requirements of this International Standard. The quality manual shall include or make reference to the quality system procedures and outline the structure of the documentation used in the quality system. | • Shall be a documented quality system<br>• Shall have an object called a "quality manual"<br>• The quality manual shall:<br>—include or make reference to the procedures<br>—outline the structure of the system |

**Note:**
If you are not working to ISO 9001/2, find the portion of the standard or code or regulation you are working to that outlines the requirements for the documented system and use it as the basis.

## The "Traditional" System

A traditional quality system design has grown up over the years, and there's a very good chance the auditor will find a variation of this system no matter where they look. The traditional model is often depicted as a triangle or pyramid, as in Figure 5–1.

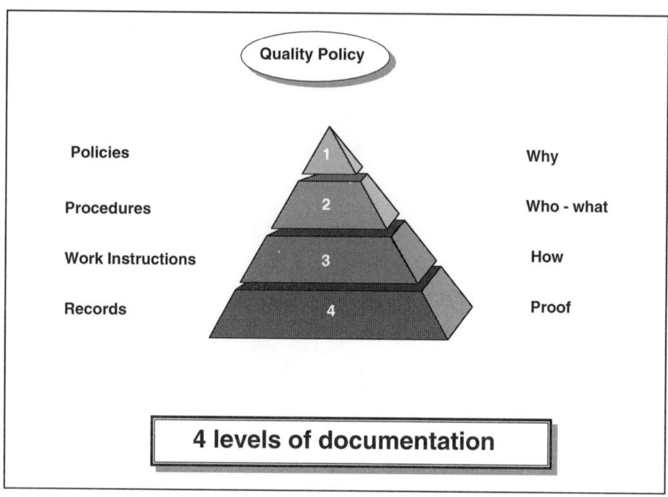


**Figure 5–1** The traditional documented system

The traditional documented system usually has four levels or "tiers." The levels are based upon the purpose of the document. They do not necessarily imply a separate volume, and sometimes the levels are combined. They have a different purpose or objective. They do different things.

## Level one—policy documents

If this is a separate volume, as it is in most cases, this volume is a "policy manual." It explains what the company stands for, what its commitment is and what its objectives are (Figure 5–2). These documents, when they are stand-alone documents, are often short and sweet and to the point. Sometimes they are direct translations of the standard or code they are written to (Table 5–2).

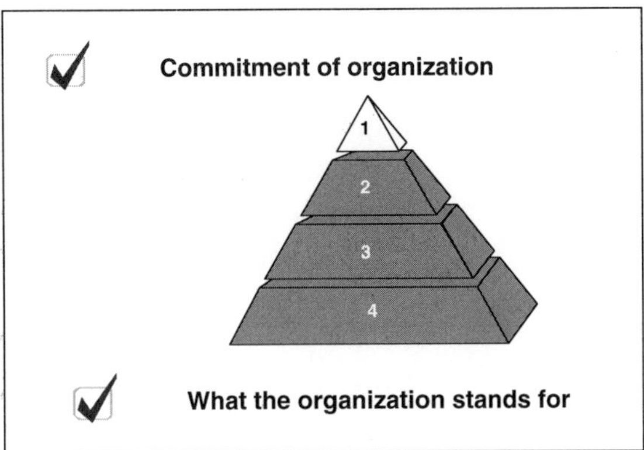


**Figure 5–2** Policy documents

**Table 5–2** A direct translation

| Standard Requirement | Policy Statement |
|---|---|
| 4.4.1 General<br><br>The supplier shall establish and maintain documented procedures to control and verify the design of the product in order to ensure that the specified requirements are met. | Section 2<br>Design Control<br><br>Designs at the ABC Company are controlled and verified to ensure that specified requirements are met. This is done in accordance with documented procedures. |

If the company has written a policy manual in this manner, the document review is fairly straightforward. There must be a policy statement for each of the requirements of the applicable standard. So the review is a direct correlation between the requirements of the standard and the policy manual. This is not always the case, however. There are times when companies have taken more indirect approaches to this manual. The reviewer needs to read the manual carefully, looking for the interpolation of the requirements.

## Level two—procedures

These are often described as a "broad-brush" view of how a company does business (Figure 5–3). The easiest way to describe them is the language shown in the diagram: "Who does what and when." If they are stand-alone documents, they are often pretty simple and direct (Table 5–3).

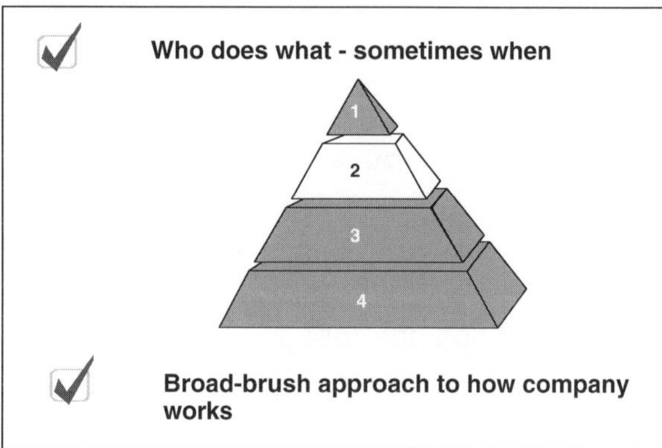


**Figure 5–3** Procedures

**Table 5–3** Policy-Procedure

| Policy Statement | Procedure |
|---|---|
| (From 4.6.3 Purchasing) | (Excerpt from procedure) |
| The supplier shall review and approve purchasing documents for adequacy of the specified requirements prior to release. | The Senior Buyer reviews and approves all purchase documents prior to release. |

## Level three—work instructions

These are the instructions for how to do specific tasks (Figure 5–4), such as reviewing the purchase order mentioned above. They may take many forms, depending on the task, the environment, and so forth. In the case of reviewing the purchase documents discussed previously, it may be in the form of a checklist, as shown in Table 5–4.

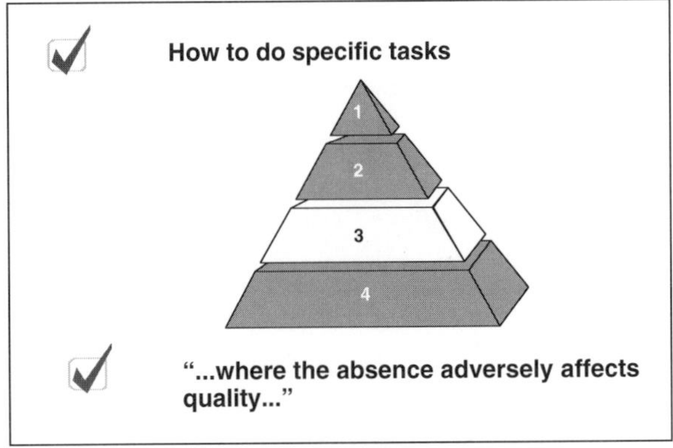


**Figure 5–4** Work instructions

**Table 5–4** Work instruction

| Purchase Document Review |
|---|
| 1. Vendor information completed? |
| 2. Is the item clearly and completely identified and described? |
| 3. Is the pricing information complete and accurate? |
| 4. Has the purchase been approved by the responsible department? |

### Level four—records

Records are proof that the system is being used and it is working (Figure 5–5).

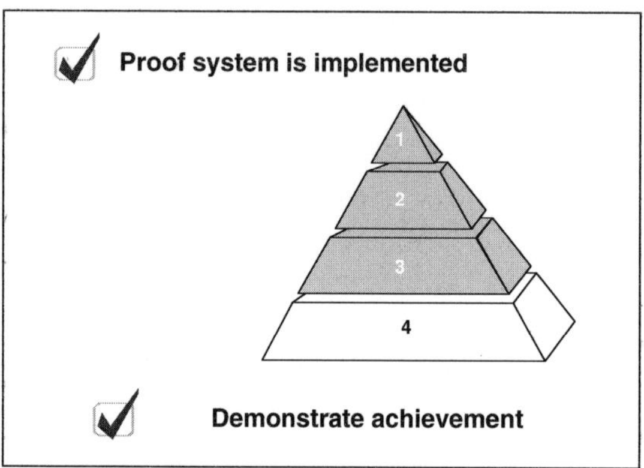


**Figure 5–5** Records

What documents the auditor has available for the adequacy audit may vary from company to company, from job to job, and from system to system. Usually, it is only the top-level document, the level-one document. If this is all the documentation the auditor has to review, the auditor should go to the portion that explains the system, and understand the structure of the system.

## Reviewing the System

The matrix that was constructed in the previous chapter can be adapted for use with any criteria the auditor is comparing the documented system to. A complete matrix to ISO 9001 was included at the end of the previous chapter.

With such a matrix, it is simple—but not necessarily easy—to review the system, point-by-point.

- The references are very important. Later they will provide the auditor a skeleton key to system
- When anything in the documentation is unclear or contradictory, note it in the "Comments" column.
- Do not jump to conclusions. Although every aspect of the applicable standard should be addressed in the top level document, the auditor may find links to lower level documentation. For example, the ISO 9001/2 standard requires that management reviews be held at "...defined intervals...". In the level-one document, it may say something like: *"Management reviews are held according to documented procedure."* This lets the auditor know there is a procedure. The exact interval may not be stated in the quality manual, and the auditor must dig up the procedure.

## Summary

In addition to being able to judge if a documented system meets the requirements of the applicable standard, when the Adequacy Audit Matrix is completed, it will serve as the beginnings of the compliance audit. (The complete form is included as part of the previous chapter.)

Once the auditor is assured the quality system meets the requirements of the applicable standard, it's time to find out if the system is actually being used.

CHAPTER 6

# Conducting the Compliance Audit

## Introduction

Remember, the purpose of a compliance audit is looking for compliance to the documented system. During the adequacy audit, the auditor was seeing if the documented system met the requirements of the applicable standard. During the compliance audit, the auditor will see if the organization is *complying* with its documented system, that is: is the organization doing what it said it would do.

Before the auditor conducts the compliance audit, he or she has built an audit plan using the applicable procedures and instructions, as we saw in chapter four. The auditor already knows what to look for when he or she arrives. Now the auditor has to talk with people, encourage others to talk with them, so, it isn't hard to see that this type of audit requires more of the auditor's communication skills then the adequacy audit. The elements of the audit remain the same.

## Gathering information

The auditor actually began gathering information when he or she studied the organization's quality system. The organization's policies and procedures are the "known criteria." The auditor has become familiar with the system and its requirements before hitting the ground.

Once the auditor has entered the workplace, the primary information gathering tools become:

- *Observing* work flow, how people do their jobs, etc.;
- *Listening* to people tell about how they do their job, what they do; and
- *Reading* any other documentation that people use to do their jobs.

## Communication skills

Strong demands are placed upon the auditor's *communication* skills during the compliance audit. This audit involves talking and interacting with people, seeing what they do, listening to what they say. And, when the audit is completed, the auditor must record the results. So it wouldn't hurt to do a little review of communication.

A good working definition of communication is that it is "...an exchange of information." That's pretty basic and neutral. There's no comment upon what the information is. It can be an opinion, or knowledge, perhaps an idea, or maybe just a point of view. What the information is doesn't matter, the elements of the basic communication model don't change. The model remains the same (Figure 6–1).

Communication models are like noses—everybody's got one—but they all basically contain the same elements as the one I've chosen.

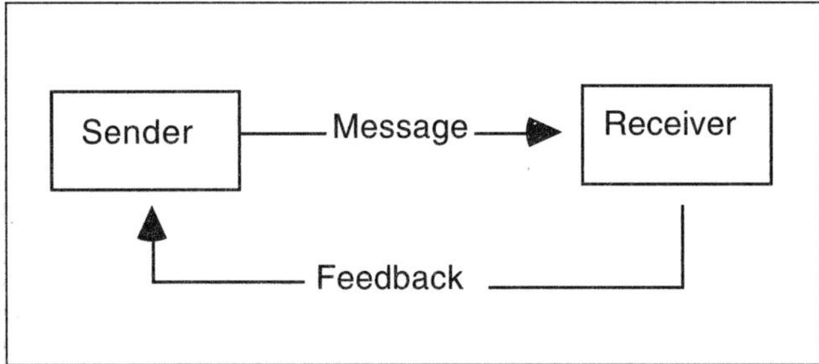


**Figure 6–1** Communication model

- Sender—this is the person who sends the message. The sender says, writes, or does something.
- Message—this is what the sender has sent, the words that were spoken or written, or the sign that was given.
- Receiver—this is the person for whom the message is intended.
- Feedback—the reaction of the person who got the message

For the exchange of information to have occurred—for communication to have happened—all four of these elements must be present. It is the idea of the exchange that is important. Without it there is no communication—or no objective evidence of communication.

There have been some models where the feedback loop has been eliminated, but there is no communication without feedback. There is no evidence that communication has taken place without feedback. If the feedback loop is eliminated, we have the classic poser: "If a tree falls in the forest and no one is there to hear it, does it make a sound?" Scientifically, yes, the sound is created, but there is no objective evidence. No one heard it.

If you don't believe in the importance of feedback, eliminate the feedback loop. You will quickly learn of its importance. This makes for a fascinating exercise.

- Make a simple drawing of boxes, something like Figure 6–2.
- Give the drawing to a person and have them stand behind a screen so they cannot be seen and have them describe the drawing to someone else.
- Have the listeners draw what the person describes. They cannot ask any questions, and the person can't say anything that would help—only describe the drawing. The listeners must draw what is described as best they can.

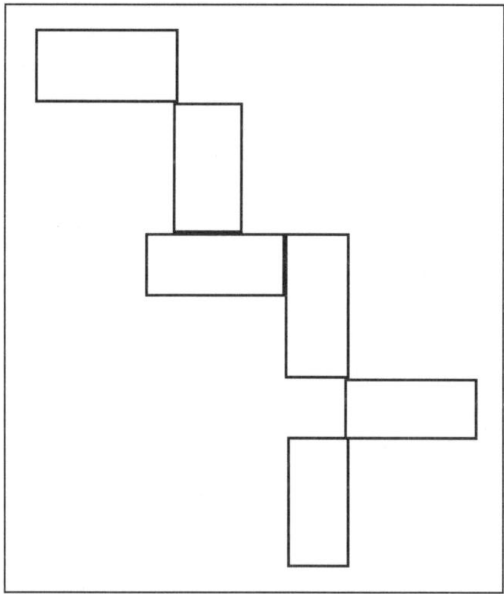

**Figure 6–2** Feedback exercise

The drawings that come out of this exercise are interesting, to say the least.

Now give the person another drawing, similar to the first, and have them stand in front of the group and describe it for the group to draw. Allow the group to ask questions this time, encourage feedback. The drawings will now more closely resemble the original.

This exercise emphasizes the importance of feedback. The first part of the exercise does not eliminate feedback—the drawings are done—but it does restrict it. This is, perhaps, the more important point. Feedback cannot be eliminated, but it can be limited or restricted. There is a very important rule here:

> *The more feedback is restricted or limited, the clearer the original message must be—if the communication is to be effective.*

We have all been guilty of restricting or limiting feedback. Have you ever heard a parent say to a child: "Now, just what do you think you were doing, and I don't want to hear a word out of you!" That throws a very serious obstacle in the feedback loop, doesn't it? But it doesn't eliminate it, does it? There's plenty of feedback in the posture of the child, in the angry or hurt expression, in the glare of the eyes.

It is important to stress the relationship between feedback and the clarity of the original message. In a military situation where feedback is restricted—the order is given and it must be carried out without question— officers and noncommissioned officers are trained to give clear, simple orders. There are plenty of examples from military history where original orders were unclear, with disastrous results. Most of us are familiar with Alfred Lord Tennyson's poem, "The Charge of the Light Brigade," which commemorates the loss of the Light Brigade during the Crimean war. Written orders were sent to the commander of the Light Brigade—a light cavalry unit—and they seemed to order a charge into the mouths of Russian cannon batteries. The order was given, no one questioned it, the charge was made, and the Light Brigade was almost annihilated. If better feedback had been possible, questions could have been asked, the orders could have been clarified and the Light Brigade could have been spared, and we would never have had "Into the valley of death rode the 600..."

During the audit interview, the auditor must ensure that the feedback loop is open and unobstructed, and should be very alert to any signs of misunderstanding. Most people do pretty well in a conversation, which is what an audit interview is, but some have difficulty with the written word. The auditor is going leave behind a written record of the results of the audit. The expected feedback is corrective action initiated for all noncompliances. The auditor may not be around when the feedback action starts, so the written words the auditor leaves behind must be clear. We will talk more about this later in the chapter on reporting the audit.

What the auditor should be very alert to are any barriers to communication. Barriers are obstructions that may arise during the original message or in the feedback. Some examples are:

- Environmental conditions. Noise, temperature, etc. These things can certainly restrict the message or the feedback.
- Language barriers. The auditor's message cannot be understood, nor can the feedback if the auditor does not understand or communicate in the same language as the other person.
- Cultural differences. Different cultures view the same thing in different ways. Should the auditor not be aware of cultural differences, the message won't be heard and understood.
- Gender/age differences. It's well known that men and women use the same words to mean different things. The message can get completely lost if the sender is not aware of these differences.

> Recently, a man asked his teenage son to "...turn the bolt counter-clockwise" and he got a questioning look back. Why? In this age of digital watches and clocks, the boy was unfamiliar with the term counter-clockwise.
>
> A college professor regaled his statistics class with a magazine article that used demographics to prove Tricia Nixon Cox (President Nixon's daughter) and Janis Joplin (a blues singer) were the same person. His mischief fell on deaf ears because no one in his class knew who either person was!
>
> The point of these two anecdotes is to emphasize the importance of the age difference. The use of analogies or examples must be relevant to the audience or they become barriers to effective communication.

If auditors are to communicate effectively, they must be alert to any barriers that can get in the way of their message or of their hearing and understanding the feedback.

## Initial phase

For a second- or third-party audit, the first activity after the auditors arrive on site is an opening meeting, or an arrival meeting. This is a formal meeting. The leader of the assessment team—the lead assessor or lead auditor—chairs this meeting. The management team of the organization being audited is expected to be present as well as the entire audit team and guides for the auditors. This meeting lasts anywhere from 15 to 30 minutes. During this meeting, everyone is introduced, the team leader goes over the schedule for the audit, confirms all the arrangements and explains the methods and procedures to be followed.

There isn't the time nor the necessity for anything this formal for an internal audit. But—and this is the important point—the same objectives must be accomplished. That is, for an internal audit the auditor must do the same things that are done at a formal open meeting. So, whether it is informal or formal, during the initial phase of the audit (or assessment) these things must be accomplished.

First get everyone introduced. The auditor—or the team—and the people being audited should introduce themselves to each other. Names, titles, and functions should be exchanged. There should be handshakes all around. If it is proper, business cards should be given out. The first thing that should happen is that everybody gets to know each other, to put names to faces and vice versa. If it is pertinent, background information on both the auditor and the people being audited should be covered.

Take the mystery out of the audit. There should be no mystery to this process, no secrets. It is up to the team leader to take the mystery out of the process. The meeting should cover:

### The *general purpose* of auditing

The auditor should always remind the person being audited about the general purpose of auditing. This is one of the biggest misconceptions people have about auditing. It is still held that the auditors are out to find where you are in error and get you punished. This isn't the general purpose of quality auditing and it isn't the attitude the auditor should have. The general purpose of auditing can be stated:

> *"The purpose of this audit is not to criticize or to blame. It is to discover the extent to which our (your) procedures are being complied with, and to recognize the need for change."*

It doesn't have to be that formal. This same idea can be given shortly and simply as:

> *"Remember, I'm not auditing the people; I'm auditing the system."*

The reason for stating the general purpose of a quality audit is to depersonalize it. Take the personal edge off the auditor, the threat that the auditor is somehow a part of a personnel appraisal system. And it doesn't hurt to say this over and over again, even though the person being audited has heard it all before. The auditor should reinforce it every time he or she conducts an audit

### The *specific purpose* of the this audit

This may be as simple as:

> *"As you know, this is a regularly scheduled internal audit."*
>
> or
>
> *"We've got a customer coming in next week, and we just wanted to check how ready we are for this customer audit."*

The auditor should let the people know why he or she is there.

### The *scope* of the audit

What is the auditor going to be looking at? How deep a look is the auditor going to take? How wide?

### The *criteria* to be used

What criteria is the audit based on? The auditor should state clearly what criteria he or she has used to plan the audit:

> *"I'm going to be auditing you to QAP #3, issue 2, dated March of this year."*

There is more to this than just stating the documentation. The auditor should get agreement from the person being audited that this is, indeed, the same documentation they are currently working to. It is not uncommon with dynamic systems for the auditor to plan an audit on one set of documentation only to find the people are working to another. When this happens, the auditor shouldn't panic. It is highly unlikely the differences are great, but the auditor should get hold of the documentation they are working to immediately and study it.

### The *method* of the audit

The auditor should tell the person being audited about how the audit is going to be conducted. This may include an explanation of the audit plan.

> *"I went through your procedure and picked out those things I wanted to look at, and I put them on this plan. This is my plan for the audit."*

And the particular activities the auditor is going to be doing.

> *"I'm going to be asking you and your people some questions about how you do your jobs. I'll want to look at records, and I'll ask you for those. I may ask to watch you or someone else do something..."*

And, out of respect for open communication, the auditor may explain about note-taking.

> *"I'll be taking notes from time to time, don't worry about them. They are just for my purposes. I'm not writing down where you're doing something wrong. I'm just making a note for me to check up on something."*

### Ask for *questions, clarity,* and *understanding*

The auditor should make sure the person being audited understands all this and is clear about it before going on. And the auditor should answer any questions the person has at this time.

> *"This all sound all right to you? Is it clear? Do you have any questions before we go on?"*

## Opening gambit

The opening gambit is how the auditor opens up the audit. It could be included in the introductory remarks, but it is important enough to be considered separately. The opening gambit is carefully chosen—and may differ from audit subject to audit subject. It is carefully considered and selected to establish rapport with and to elicit open communication from the audit subject. The auditor is trying to put the subject at ease, to get them comfortable enough so they will speak freely and openly. That is the reason behind the auditor going through all the steps of the initial phase—taking all the mystery out of the audit—so the person feels more easy about it. In spite of the auditor's best efforts during the initial phase, there still might be an edge to the situation, and the opening gambit is needed to take the sharpness off that edge.

Shared miseries are good opening gambits. We all have to contend with the weather, traffic, and other assaults on are well being. Sometimes the best opening is to simply let the audit subject know that you suffer as they do.

> *"How about that traffic this morning? Did you come in on the freeway? I don't know how we're going to make things better."*
>
> or
>
> *"Wasn't that a great weekend?"*

A key when using this opening is to keep the comments general. It has the results of making the auditor seem human, as human as the subject—after all, I had to drive the same freeway; I barbecued in the backyard yesterday—but it has to be handled gently or it can turn into a "bitch session." Those can get mean-spirited, and they can take away from the thrust of the audit.

Another good method of getting started is to discuss shared interests. Such things as sports or hobbies are a high passion to a lot of individuals, and they will talk readily about them.

*"Did you watch the game yesterday?"*

or

*"Do you think they are going to take the championship this year?"*

However, a couple of words of caution:

- Don't get into an argument. The auditor should ensure that he or she and the subject are fans of the same team. Coming into an audit rooting for a rival team can certainly redirect the focus of the audit somewhere the auditor doesn't want it to be.
- Don't fake it. There is nothing more aggravating than someone trying to impress you with meaningless observations and statistics when they don't understand anything about them.

  If the auditor doesn't know anything about the sport or the hobby, the auditor may use this to an advantage. Admit ignorance and get the audit subject to start talking about it. Once I noticed photos of an audit subject with hunting trophies on his desk. I am not a hunter, but I got him to talking about turkey hunting—it was turkey season—and he happily told me of the thrill and challenge of the hunt. He was glad to share this information with me. I'm still not a hunter and I did not have to promise to go turkey hunting with him, but the communication channels were open. He was talking.

One very effective gambit is what I call "helpless in my ignorance." This opening gambit is used by a lot of experienced auditors and can be extremely effective because it appears as a cry for help. Coupled with this cry for help is a sly pat on the back and an ego trigger. The "helpless in my ignorance" gambit may go something like this.

> *"I gotta tell you, I read through your procedures last night, and I'm impressed. You have a big job. This is quite a department. But, I gotta be honest with you, I don't know that I truly understand what all goes on here. So, I wonder, before we really get going with the audit, if you could just take a few minutes and explain to me what actually happens here."*

This may appear to some as being duplicitous. It isn't really, because, remember, the purpose of this opening gambit is to open up the communication, put the subject at ease and get them talking. Most people like to talk about their job—they may feel they are underpaid, overworked and undervalued. They are more than willing to talk about what they actually do.

There is a danger in this. The auditor must control this part of the audit very carefully and not let it get away. This should not take up a lot of time. Remember, the auditor's goal is complete the scope of the audit, and good time management is critical in the process. The auditor may be successful in priming the pump and getting the audit subject to talking, but the auditor has got to control the conversation. When the subject starts talking freely, the auditor's effort becomes one of channeling the conversation in the direction he or she wants it to go.

Once, two neophyte auditors asked a mechanical CAD/CAM manager a single question, and they were inundated with information. This manager was very enthusiastic. He had nothing to hide and he wanted to share everything about his department. He did. He talked and talked and talked. He talked so much the two auditors hardly got to ask another question. The information came at a flood rate and they were overwhelmed. They lost control of the audit. This can happen to any auditor, if the auditor doesn't exert—re-exert—his or her control over the audit.

*"That's fascinating, and I would like to talk about that, but maybe later. Right now, I'm interested in..."*

## Asking Questions

The introductory portion is over. The auditor has gotten the subject relaxed and talking, the audit proper is in motion. The primary tool for moving the audit along is the question. Auditing, after all, is often merely an interview. The success or failure often depends upon the type and quality of the questions.

### Closed questions

Questions that can logically, legitimately be answered "yes" or "no" are called *closed questions.* These are questions that have the intransitive verbs as stems: "Do you...?", "Are you...?", "Can you...?"

*"Do you have a procedure for that?"*

*"Are you the person who does that?"*

*"Can you do that alone?"*

All of these questions can be answered with a simple "yes" or "no," and none of them will get the auditor the depth of information needed. These sort of questions can take up a lot of time and leave the auditor short on information.

Most of us at one time or another have played the simple children's game called Hangman. A scaffold is drawn and blanks are put along the lower part of the paper. The blanks represent a word. The object for the players is to guess the letters that make up the word. For every correct guess a letter is placed in its appropriate blank. For every incorrect guess, a portion of a hanged person is put on the scaffold, the head, the body, arms, legs, etc. The popular television show "Wheel of Fortune" is a version of this game. The frustrating thing about this game is that the questions are restricted to closed questions. Every "yes" answer gets a letter; every "no" answer gets the player closer to being hanged. The number of questions the player can ask is determined by how many parts are added before he or she is "hanged." When a player gets "hanged," they realize the weakness in the closed question. They simply do not get enough information.

For this reason, a lot of people will say to forget about closed questions altogether, declaring "They are a waste of time." I don't think so. I think they have their place, used sparingly. Actually, a lot of times, they can be used to put an audit subject at ease. When asked a simple closed question, they answer it quickly and feel better. On the auditors' part, they should realize they have asked a closed question, they are not going to get a lot of information and have another question right behind it as a follow up.

All of us have found ourselves in a situation where we see a person with a watch on their wrist and we ask them: "Excuse me, can you tell me what time it is?"

They look at us, perhaps look at their watch, nod and say "Yes." And they hurry away, leaving us with the urge to kill.

The fault doesn't lie with the answer. The person answered the question asked. "Yes, I have a watch. Yes, I can read it. Yes, I can tell you what time it is." The fault lies in the question. We asked the wrong question. Instead of asking "Can you tell me what time it is?", we should have asked:

*"Excuse me, what time is it?"*

## Open questions

*"Excuse me, what time is it?"*

This is an example of an open question. Open questions are those questions that cannot—logically and legitimately—be answered with a simple "yes" or "no." If you asked someone what time it is, and they nod and say "yes," the fault is not in the question but in the relative sanity—or understanding—of the person answering.

Open questions have the stems shown in Table 6–1.

**Table 6–1** Open questions

| Stem | Example |
|---|---|
| Who | *"Who is responsible for doing that?"* |
| Where | *"Where are those kept when they're not being used?"* |
| What | *"What happens next?"* |
| When | *"When does the inspector look at the product?"* |
| How | *"How are you sure the operator has the correct version of the document?"* |
| Why | *"Why are the components marked like that?"* |

Each of the questions in Table 6–1 requires more of an answer than a simple "yes" or "no." The answers may be short, for example:

*"Who is responsible for doing that?"*

may get the auditor a shrug and a:

*"I dunno."*

but this tells the auditor a lot. It tells the auditor that this organization has not done a very good job of defining authority and responsibility, if nothing more. At least, it has opened some doors the closed question wouldn't have.

A note of caution needs to be raised about "why" questions. They can sometimes imply criticism: For example a question like this…

*"Why do you do that that way?"*

...might seem as if you're implying, "That's a dumb way of doing that." But don't avoid the "why" questions—they are perfectly good and important questions—just be careful how you phrase the question, and the tone in your voice. Don't make the question a comment on how they are doing their work.

Open questions such as these are the auditor's primary tools in the information-gathering business. They are the shovels and spades, the earth movers, so to speak. They scrape away the covering and get to the information beneath the surface. The auditor should use open questions most of the time during the interview.

Sometimes this is difficult because we are very prone to asking closed question. We do it in our everyday conversation all the time. During an audit, the auditor has to be very aware of the questions he or she is asking, catch themselves asking closed questions and try to convert them into open questions (Table 6–2).

**Table 6–2** Question conversion

| Closed Question | Open Question |
|---|---|
| *"Do you have a procedure for that?* | *"Where is your procedure?"* |
| *"Are you responsible for that?"* | *"Who is responsible for that?"* |
| *"Can you stop production if you discover a trend toward poor quality?"* | *"Who can stop production when a trend toward poor quality is discovered?"* |
| *"Is there record kept of that?"* | *"What kind of record is kept of that?"* |

## Linking questions

Sometimes the auditor may decide that a closed question is the proper choice at a precise moment. This may be because of the audit subject's discomfort. If the auditor uses a closed question, he or she should have a follow-up question already prepared and waiting.

This follow-up question should be an open question. The exchange may go like this:

- Closed question:

  *"Do you keep copies of purchase orders?"*
- Answer

  *"Yes."*
- Open question—follow up

  *"Where do you keep them?"*

This a natural, easy order should the auditor use a closed question as a starting point. The affirmative answer leads to the open question, which will lead the evidence. But there is one more step to take.

## Show me—"the auditor's imperative"

One the most important information-gathering tools the auditor has is the use of the imperative, or directive, "show me." This generally gets the auditor *objective evidence*. What is objective evidence?

> "Objective evidence is the qualitative or quantitative information, records, or statements of fact pertaining to the quality of an item or service or to the existence and implementation of a quality system element, which is based on observation, measurement, or test, and which can be verified." (ISO 8402)

"Show me" is not a demand—the auditor is trying to encourage communication, remember? The auditor won't get any information if he or she is rude or impolite.

"Show me" is often stated as a closed question, in the polite form.

*"May I see..."*

*"Could you show me..."*

*"Would you show me on those, please?"*

What "show me" is asking for is something to be put in the auditor's hands, or something to be done so the auditor may observe. It is, so to speak, the proof of the pudding. It might work like this:

- Closed question:

  *"Do you keep copies of purchase orders?"*
- Answer

  *"Yes."*
- Open question—follow up

  *"Where do you keep them?"*
- Show me

  *"May I see purchase order number 6085, Please?"*

## Some questions to avoid

Since we have been talking about effective questioning, it only makes sense to discuss some of the types of questions the auditor should avoid.

### Leading questions

These are questions that indicate how they are to be answered.

*"You meet the requirements of ISO 9001, don't you?"*

Leading questions are for people who already know the answer. If the auditor already knew the answer to the question, he or she wouldn't be auditing. There wouldn't be any need to audit. The only positive value leading questions might have for you as an auditor is to check for your understanding.

*"Before you go on, let me make sure I understand what you just told me. You said you do A, B, and C, is that right?"*

### Multiple questions

This is when two are more questions are strung together and are asked at the same time.

*"Who prepares and controls this document?"*

There are really two questions here, and—maybe—two answers. Asking more than one question just confuses the issue. When auditors catch questions piling up in their heads, they should slow down, separate the questions and ask them one at a time.

### Hypothetical questions

These are questions that deal with fantasy or "what ifs." They do not get the required factual information.

*"What would happen if a flying saucer landed here?"*

Questions that have their origin in the documents of the company are not hypothetical. For example, if the company stated they would use a quality plan to deal with customer requirements that exceed those of their quality system, it would be perfectly legitimate to ask:

*"I see you say you would use a quality plan for any customer requirements that exceed your own. Has that ever happened?"*

If the answer is "Yes, we've done that," then you may ask to see one of the those quality plans. If the answer is "No, that's never come up," then let it go. To pursue it any further is hypothetical.

### Questioning summary

The best type of questions to ask are open questions: They get the most information. Closed questions may be used to open doors or to lead into areas, but they don't get a lot of information and should be used sparingly. Avoid leading questions, avoid combining questions, and don't ask hypothetical questions.

One of the things that makes auditing a difficult activity is that you have to remain focused on the conversation. You have to be very conscious of every question you ask. You can't just relax into the conversation like you do with your friends.

But asking questions and being aware of them is not enough.

## Listening

The auditor may ask the most wonderful questions in the world and still not conduct an effective audit. The auditor may not get any information—which is the auditor's job—because the auditor didn't listen to the answers. Asking wonderful questions doesn't get any information. Listening to the answers is what gets the auditor information.

Some wag once said that an auditor has two eyes, two ears, and one mouth, and they should be used in those proportions. Which means the auditor ought to be quiet most of the time.

Listening is both one of the simplest and one of the most difficult of all communication skills. The reason it is so difficult is that everybody thinks they're already very good at it. We've been listening all our lives, so we must be doing it right. It's rather like breathing. Everyone thinks they are an expert at breathing. They must be because they are still alive. It isn't until a person takes a speech or singing class do they suddenly discover they have been breathing wrong...well, breathing inefficiently at any rate. Listening is pretty much the same way. It is a simple skill, but one that we must acknowledge we probably aren't doing as efficiently as we should be.

You not only have to hear the words, you must also hear *how* the words are said and you must also listen for the things *not said*.

A simple way of putting this is that the effective listener listens for the *facts* and the *truth*—which are sometimes not the same thing. For example, when asked if they ever vary from a procedure, an audit subject may say something like:

*"Oh, no, we never take chances with that kind of thing."*

The facts are clearly stated: they do not take chances with that kind of thing. The truth may be different. The effective listener hears *how* that statement is made.

*"Oh, no, we never take chances with that kind of thing."*

If the emphasis is placed on *that*, it could indicate a truth—a truth the audit subject is not saying:

*"We've taken chances with other kinds of things."*

The effective listener hears that and immediately follows it up. The ineffective listener misses the entire exchange and only hears the facts.

We human beings prize our ability with language. We are the only animal in the world that uses language to communicate. There are some who believe that dolphins have a capacity for language, but I don't believe the evidence is in to prove this conclusively. A lot of animals use sound to communicate, but not language. The sounds are not clumped into abstract symbols that can communicate complex thoughts and ideas. And some of us are bilingual, which is even more amazing. The bilingual person can understand two abstract sets of symbols!

As much as we pride ourselves on our language abilities, some studies have shown that we only get something like ten percent of our messages through the actual meaning of the words. *Ten Percent*! We get approximately thirty percent of our message through sound—*how* the words are spoken. You can see this in practice when speaking to a prelanguage child or a pet. They do not respond to the meaning of the words. They respond to the sound of the voice. You can say "I love you" in a harsh tone of voice and the child or pet will respond to the harsh tone—not the words.

The effective listener must listen and hear both. Take a simple sentence made up of simple words.

*"I didn't tell you to put that there."*

We can all read the sentence, but we don't know what it really means until we hear it in context. This simple sentence can have many meanings, depending upon how it is said, as is shown in Table 6–3.

**Table 6–3** Different meanings depending upon emphasis

| Emphasis | Meaning |
|---|---|
| *I* didn't tell you to put that there. | Some one else told you |
| I *didn't* tell you to put that there. | No such order was given |
| I didn't *tell* you to put that there. | I might have thought it, but I didn't tell it |
| I didn't tell *you* to put that there. | I told someone else |
| I didn't tell you *to* put that there. | Denial, again... |
| I didn't tell you to *put* that there. | I meant throw it, not put it |
| I didn't tell you to put *that* there. | I meant something else, not that |
| I didn't tell you to put that *there*. | I meant here and not there |

All those meanings can come from that one sentence, depending where the emphasis is placed. The effective listener has to hear the differences.

Hearing what *isn't* said requires another information gathering tool—and it is connected to that other sixty percent of our messages.

## Nonverbal forms of communication

If we get ten percent of our messages through the meaning of words and thirty percent of our messages through the sound, where does the other sixty percent of our messages come from? From all the other forms of communication that do not rely upon our voice and our language.

### Eye contact

This is the single-most important form of nonverbal communication in our society, and in most other western societies. We do not trust people who do not look us in the eye, and we cannot establish and generate trust in others if we do not look them in the eye.

Successful communicators establish eye contact early and then work hard at maintaining it. They are very aware when they are breaking eye contact, such as when they want to make a note. They often let the person being audited know how much they value the eye contact, by saying something like:

*"Excuse me, I want to make a note of that."*

In addition to establishing trust, eye contact is essential to truly understanding the communication from the person being audited. The person may answer a question one way, but the eyes may be saying something else, such as confusion, lack of understanding or even fear.

The successful communicator is also aware of cultural differences and does not expect someone of another culture to act or react like someone of this culture. In some Oriental and Mideastern cultures it is considered impolite to look a stranger directly in the eye. This is disturbing to some Americans when dealing with people from these other cultures, and it disturbing because we don't trust people who don't look us in the eyes! This just reinforces the observation that eye contact is important to us as a culture.

When conducting an audit in this country—and in Mexico, as I understand—establish eye contract quickly and maintain it through the audit.

### Facial expression

Human beings are blessed with very expressive features. We smile, grimace, look grim, set our jaw, furrow our brow, squint our eyes, all with this wonderful feature, our face. Effective communicators are sensitive to facial expression.

### Body language

There has been a growth industry in the study and interpretation of body language over recent years. Some of the work has been very valuable in helping us interpret and understand human behavior, and some has been superficial and erroneous. If a person relies on the interpretation of body language as a primary tool, they will be wrong as often as if they had used astrology. But body language can't be ignored. An effective communicator is sensitive to how the person is standing, how their shoulders and head are held, where the person is looking, what the person does with their hands, and so on. It may not give the auditor full understanding of their mind, of what they are thinking, but it does offer some insight, and the auditor may use this insight as a clue.

### Gestures

People use their hands to express themselves, some more than others. The gestures can be simple and direct like a finger point or more subtle and complex, such as rubbing the back of the neck. The effective auditor watches the hands and follows them in their movements, looking for clues to lead him or her to the truth.

### Clothing

The way people dress is a form of nonverbal communication. It is of minimal value to the auditor, but it will give the auditor clues to other aspects of the person he or she is examining.

#### Space

The distance we keep from each other, our *space*, is another method we have of communicating nonverbally. Again, there are cultural differences here. Some cultures like to stay apart, and some are more comfortable being closer.

## Setting up the Audit

All right, let's see if we can pull this stuff together and walk through an audit.

### Dressing the part

How does the auditor dress for an audit? Is there a prescribed dress? The auditor should consider a lot of things when dressing for an audit.

#### Comfort

First of all, what is comfortable for the auditor? If the auditor is going to make the audit subject comfortable, then the auditor should be comfortable. If the auditor is stiff and uncomfortable, that can't help but interfere with the successful completion of the audit.

#### Convention

The auditor must take into account the conventions of the area they are auditing. As casual as we might all like to be, there are certain areas and companies where being casual is taken as a sign of a lack of professionalism. So auditors must measure their own comfort with the conventions of the area or company they are auditing in.

#### Environment

The auditor has to consider the environment. There are environments where a suit and a tie are not appropriate, and can actually become an obstacle. If the audit is to be conducted in a machine shop where there is dirty air, the audit subjects will worry about the auditor's nice clothes more than they will listen to the auditor's questions. There are times when hard-toe shoes are required, when high heels cannot be worn, when jewelry is forbidden, when arms and legs must be completely covered...and then there are clean rooms where it really doesn't matter how the auditor is dressed under the clean-room garb.

## Equipment, material, and supplies

Actually auditing is one of those activities where there is an absolute minimum of required equipment, materials and supplies. Let's discuss some possibilities.

### Tape recorders

I cannot tell you how many times I have been asked about the advisability of using one of the small micro-recorders for audits. My advice always has been—and will likely continue to be—don't use one. People are always intimidated by recorders. The presence of a recorder will, in general, inhibit communication, not enhance it. So fall back on the recorder we all have: our mind and our ears.

### Clipboard

A lot of auditors like clipboards. They are used as a kind of psychological body armor—a barrier between the audit subject and auditor. If your plan is on a complete sheet of paper, that plan fits very well on a clipboard, so the clipboard becomes a good tool. You can also use it to clip a copy of the ISO standard on. Personally, I don't care for clipboards. I prefer to come into audits empty handed, but there's nothing wrong with clipboards, if you are comfortable with them.

### Tablet, note-paper

Whether or not these are useful depends entirely upon how many notes the auditor plans on taking. Hopefully, the auditor's audit plan has enough room for him or her to take notes, and he or she does not need anything more.

### Pencils, pens

Yes, the auditor will need something to write with. It boils down to what the auditor is comfortable with. There is no set rule. Remember, the auditor's notes will become part of the record of the audit.

## Setting

This is sometimes a very difficult issue because the auditor doesn't always have control over the setting for the audit. The auditor cannot always direct or pick where the audit is going to be held. Sometimes it will be in an office setting and sometimes on a factory floor depending of the audit subject. The auditor needs to talk with the audit subject in the audit subject's environment, if possible. That is where the "current activities" are happening and probably where the "recorded results" are. So it is where the audit needs to be held.

Be careful of environmental elements that can affect the audit, such as noise, dirty surfaces, or air quality. In some extreme clean room environments, outside paper or writing instruments cannot be taken inside the room. If an effective audit cannot be accomplished in the environment, the auditor may observe what can be observed and move the audit to a better environment as soon as possible. It is not unlikely for an auditor to observe a subject perform a task, then to ask them to adjourn to a nearby coffee or break room for a conversation. At least the auditor can have a conversation there.

If the environment is suitable for the audit, the auditor needs to consider other things:

### Position

The auditor should be where he or she can establish and maintain good eye contact with the subject and in a place that is comfortable for the subject. Sometimes across the subject's desk is good. It provides a head-on view of the auditor and the subject. The auditor—or the subject—might feel the desk is too much separation; there is too much distance. Subjects will sometimes come around and sit in front of the desk with the auditor. This is often comfortable and affords good eye contact.

A recent study predicts that given two chairs, men will most often position themselves in direct confrontation. That is, they will position the two chairs facing each other. On the other hand, women will tend to put the chairs side by side. Don't make too much of this, but remember it when your audit subject is a female and there are two chairs. She might be more comfortable with the chairs side by side. This isn't carved in stone anywhere, but it's something to keep in mind when auditing. The subject should be as comfortable as possible.

### Level

Wherever, the audit is held, the auditor should try to maintain the same level as the subject. If the subject is seated, the auditor should sit. The auditor who stands over a subject is intimidating and makes the subject uncomfortable. The auditor should strive to establish and maintain an equal relationship. The auditor shouldn't place him- or herself in a superior position, nor let the audit subject place them in the subordinate position. There are times when it is not possible. For example, if the subject is operating a machine, the auditor cannot control the situation. The auditor can keep the conversation to a minimum and wait until the task is complete. It should be easy to find a comfortable place to have the conversation later.

## Attitude

Quality systems auditors should come to the audit with a positive attitude. The days of the auditor being the "grim executioner" should be long over. What the quality auditor is looking for is compliance—not searching for ways to nail the audit subject. The auditor expects compliance; when noncompliances are found, they are the exception and not the rule.

The auditor should keep the audit as relaxed as possible. The auditor should remain as casual and informal as the situation allows, or make it so, if possible. If the audit subject is stiff and formal because of fear or intimidation, perhaps the auditor can lead the way into a more relaxed atmosphere. Auditing is hard work but the person being audited is working hard, too. By keeping the audit casual and informal, and as relaxed as possible, it is easier, there is more cooperation, and a better possibility of success.

## Time Management

The auditor should manage time effectively. There is never enough time for an audit. All the best planning in the world can go to pieces in a moment during an audit. Why? Because if there is one rule to auditing, it is *expect the unexpected*! The auditor just never knows what's going to happen, and needs to keep one eye on the clock and one eye on the plan.

The auditor should remember that it is his or her responsibility to cover the entire scope of the audit as directed, and should manage time so this can happen. The auditor must remember that there is a system to the audit, and that his or her audit is a part of this larger system. The results of the entire system depends upon the auditor covering the entire scope given to him or her.

## Remember the objective

The objective of the audit is to realize the scope of the audit. That's what the plan is for, and it should be the auditor's guide. What the auditor is seeking is objective evidence of compliance. When the auditor thinks he or she has found a noncompliance, they should ask some more questions, dig a little deeper, and look for more evidence to confirm it. Often auditors give up when they are told something, instead of going the next step and getting the evidence in their hands. For example, a buyer in the purchasing office may tell the auditor that product has been purchased from subcontractors who are not approved vendors. The auditor's heart may quicken, but before he or she starts writing, the auditor should ask for a particular incident where that has happened, ask to see the record, and get the record—the objective evidence—in their hands.

## Concluding the audit

When the auditor has covered the scope of the audit or when time has run out, it's time to conclude the audit. The auditor can't just pack up, say "thanks," and leave. There is the reporting function to take care of, and we'll discuss the reporting function in the next chapter. For now, let's talk about the protocol for concluding the audit.

- Leave time to record and report on the findings. Any noncompliances must be written up, and if the audit procedure requires an audit report (or summary) be completed, that should be written up. Whatever the findings, they must be reported to the person "...having responsibility in the area being audited."

  Team audits often conclude with a formal closing meeting. Individual audits often do not have the time for the formal meeting. But, whether it is a formal or an informal meeting, the points covered should be the same.
- Thank the department and staff for their support, their hospitality and their cooperation during the audit. Never leave unhappy people behind. This will not help the audit program. It will seed a minefield for the next auditor. This is where the auditor's tact and politeness

comes in hand. Say, "I want to thank everyone for their hospitality and cooperation," whether they were hospitable and cooperative or not. If they were not, take that matter up with the team leader, the company, or whoever is managing the audit program.

- Give a brief overview on the purpose and scope of the audit. The auditor should briefly review why the audit was conducted and what he or she looked at.
- Review areas actually covered during the audit. The auditor should review the areas looked into as a means of ensuring that the scope of the audit was accomplished.
- State positive points of the audit before detailing the noncompliances. The auditor should state any of the positive things he or she found during the audit. In formal meetings, for legal reasons, this is often called a "disclaimer," and it is about ensuring the principle that auditing is sampling. In a more informal setting, this simply allows the audit subject to know they are doing something right.
- Review the findings individually. The auditor should go over each of the findings individually. Read them carefully and check often for understanding. This means it is important that the auditor write their findings clearly and precisely (see Chapter 7). The auditor should look at the audit subject for the first sign of misunderstanding. And the auditor's question should never be, "Do you agree?" What the auditor has documented is objective evidence, and there is no allowance for agreement or disagreement. The question is, "Do you understand that?"
- Get acknowledgment, if required. Acknowledgment simply means, "Yes, that is true." It is not, in the words of the highway patrolman, "An admission of guilt." It simply means, I have read this and I understand it. With most systems, it is imperative the auditor get a

signature, as acknowledgment, for each noncompliance. In the case of team audits, this task may fall to the guides. In less formal audits, such as internal audits, it is done by the audit subject—the "...responsible personnel in the area being audited...," as ISO 9001/2 states. As the auditor goes over each noncompliance with the audit subject, check for understanding. If the audit subject agrees, the subject signs the form. If the audit subject doesn't agree, the auditor should find out why. If the audit subject says they simply do not understand, the auditor may rewrite and clarify the noncompliance on sight; then get a signature. If the audit subject says that they do not agree and refuse to sign, the auditor shouldn't argue. First, the auditor should find out why the subject is unwilling to sign. If they don't understand, the auditor may work with them to clarify the written statements before moving on. If they don't agree with the noncompliance, the auditor shouldn't argue. The auditor should simply say, "okay," and move on to the next. Take the noncompliance to the team leader or the audit program manager and let them deal with it.

- Leave a copy of the findings with the department. This may be appropriate in internal audits. It may not be with team audits. If it is appropriate, make a copy of the (signed) noncompliance and leave it with the audit subject. They must take corrective action.

## Summary

Experienced auditors will often say that "Auditing is hard work." This isn't just self-aggrandizement or an expression of self-pity. Auditing *is* hard work, but it is hard work because it is a focused conversation. We have conversations all the time, and most of the time they are relaxing and rejuvenating. But our conversations wander and meander. They aren't compressed and we can wander in and out of attention. Silence can be extended. Time is not a factor. Then we walk into an audit situation. Now we are having a conversation, but now time is a factor, and we must pay close attention to everything we say and everything we hear and see. Now the conversation becomes work. It is challenging and demanding.

But don't be scared off.

Auditing, as I said in the very beginning of this book, *is* a human activity. It capitalizes on the skills and abilities we have been using for most of our lives. Anyone can learn to be an effective auditor, through application and determination.

Remember our goal as an auditor is to realize the scope of the audit. We are gathering objective evidence of compliance. We do this by reading, listening, and observing. We talk to people, watch people work, and read the documentation and records of their work.

The only way we can gather the type and amount of information we need is through open and free communication with the audit subject. The subject may be nervous or intimidated by the very fact they're being audited. This puts demands on our ability to loosen them up, get them talking, and open up the channels of communication During our interview with people we are going to ask questions, and we need to ask questions that will elicit information. Generally, we are going to ask open questions, since they will get us the most information, and we will ask that the audit subject show us things or activities that will give us objective evidence of compliance. When our time is up, we will have covered the scope, we will present our results, and leave the audit subject with our thanks.

Now this sounds simple, but it is not. The thing to remember is that we can and will improve audit by audit—if we want to. We could devise a simple self-improvement program to ensure that the next audit we do will be an improvement over the one we just completed. This could be as simple as asking (and answering) these three questions:

- What did I do that worked (well)? What am I happy with? What did I do that I liked? Be honest with yourself, praise yourself, and recognize the things you did well.
- What opportunities did I miss? Again, be honest with yourself, because every time you walk away from an audit you'll know there were some things you missed, some questions you should have asked and didn't, some places you should have looked but didn't. Write these down.
- What will I do differently next time? Select one specific thing to do differently the next time you audit. Don't write something general like, "I'm gonna be better," because you won't. And don't make a list. Pick one thing and write it down.

Now, file this paper in your personal file. Next time you are assigned an audit, take it out and it will give you a plan. It is simple, and it works.

Remember:

*"The best audit I've ever done is the next one!"*

# CHAPTER 7

# Reporting on the Audit

## Introduction

All the wonderful information the auditor has gathered will not do anybody any good unless it is recorded and reported. The results of the audit need to be documented in some fashion, and then they need to be reported to those people who can do something about them. If there are noncompliances, there will need to be corrective action. If there are no noncompliances, the accolades need to be given out. All of the results, good and bad, need to be documented and reported.

To a degree, this can be one of the most difficult of all the auditor's jobs. It relies upon the auditor's writing skill, and skill at writing is not always in great abundance these days. And this writing can be confrontational. The auditor may have to inform people that things are not going as well as they should be and sometimes people can become defensive when they are told such things. No one likes to be told there is a problem. So in addition to being a good communicator and listener, the auditor must be a good writer as well.

What is good writing?

Good writing is clear, easily understood, concise, and precise. People must understand what the auditor has written because they are going to take action based on what the auditor has said.

A lot of very good internal audit programs fail because of poor recording and reporting. Very good auditors who do not have sufficient writing skills have written awful reports, containing no information or containing information so cluttered and confused that no one can work with it. The results of the audit are nothing, nada, zilch, zero.

Because writing is so important to the success of the audit program, it might be wise for us to take a little time to talk about some basic writing fundamentals.

## Writing Fundamentals

All good writing is about communication—communicating ideas, opinions, instructions, even feelings. Good business and technical writing is about the same thing: communication. This section contains some simple ideas about writing. The things in this section can be applied to any kind of writing and to any audience.

### Words

Words are the simplest building blocks of written communication, so we'll begin there.

An extensive vocabulary has long been one of the criteria of an educated, well-spoken individual. But that is too simplistic. What an extensive vocabulary does for a person is give them more tools with which to communicate better; it does not guarantee better communication. If the person uses words that are unfamiliar to his audience, the audience will not receive the message. There has been no communication. So, we don't need a lot of words—we just need the right words.

### The "right" word

Mark Twain once wrote:

> *"The difference between the almost right word and the right word is really a large matter. 'Tis the difference between the lightning bug and lightning."*

Selecting the right word means selecting the word that communicates *exactly* what you want to say. This is not always as easy as it sounds.

### Simple words

Simplicity is emphasized over and over again. And over and over again it is forgotten or abandoned. People continue to write involved, impressive tomes using impressive, large, and sometimes unfamiliar words. It is taken as a sign of erudition (like that word), sophistication, or education to use more complex words.

But often the primary objective—the exchange of information—is lost. Nothing but confusion gets exchanged.

It is said that the fifty most common words in English usage are single-syllable words. If they are the most common, that means they probably communicate the most effectively. Why not use them when we write?

Remember the slogans and mottos and old sayings we've heard all of our lives. Look at them and what do you find? Simple words.

Simple words don't just work in old adages. They have a simple, direct power no matter what your objective. Below are some examples of simple word usage from famous men.

> *"I will say: it is to wage war; by sea, land and air, with all our might and with all the strength that God can give us."*
>
> —Winston Churchill

All of the words in Mr. Churchill's famous speech are simple words, direct words, familiar words—and they are all single syllable words.

The American poet Robert Frost said:

> *"Home is the place where, when you go there, they have to take you in."*

And, here again are simple, single-syllable words used to great effect. How about this piece of motivational psychology:

> *"If it is to be, it is up to me."*
>
> —William H. Johnson

There is a professor in one of the posh prep schools who has his students write a complete essay using only single syllable words. A couple of examples have been reprinted, and they are powerful and evocative.

It might help if we thought as we wrote that we were being paid by the word and not the syllable. Twain gave us the following guideline:

> *"I never write metropolis for seven cents when I can get the same for city."*

It is not always possible to use simple, single-syllable words, but it should be our goal, and such words should be our first choice, when possible. Let's close this discussion with another quote from Twain. A young man wrote him a letter once, asking for advice about writing. This was part of his reply.

> *"I notice you use plain, simple language, short words and brief sentences. That is the way to write English—it is the modern way and the best way. Stick to it; and don't let fluff and flowers and verbosity creep in."*

## Verbs

Verbs are those action words in our language. They are words that describe what we do. There are some important fundamentals about how we use verbs.

### *Active voice*

Perhaps it is rooted in how we see ourselves as a nation, but Americans tend to respond better to the active voice. It is simpler and more direct. For example, the following statement is written in the passive voice:

> *"The entry is made by the clerk."*

It seems a little twisted, a little remote to us. We would much prefer:

> *"The clerk enters..."*

So, a good rule of thumb is to use the active voice when we write.

### *Tense*

You have often read statements like the following:

> *"The document clerk will enter..."*

This describes a prescribed action as if it is something that will happen in the future. Again, why can't we be more direct and use the present tense: do it now. The statement becomes:

> *"The document clerk enters..."*

### *Conditional verbs*

These are helping verbs that worm their way into our sentences. Often they don't help. They clutter.

*"The operator may finish the entry at this time."*

This statement is better as:

*"Finish the entry at this time."*

*Gerund and infinitive forms*

These are two verb forms that you may find very helpful in writing simple, direct, and effective prose.

The gerund form of the verb is where *'ing '* is added to the verb form, as in the example below.

*"The drive is changed and the operation is complete."*

becomes

*"Changing the drive completes the operation."*

And the statement becomes simpler. Gerund forms are sometimes effective for titles of operations, such as:

*"Operating Procedure #5—Submitting a Change"*

The infinitive form is also helpful making our prose simpler and more direct. In this simple form the helper 'to' is attached to the verb.

*"Use weights for stabilization of the internal clocking mechanism."*

becomes

*"Use weights to stabilize the internal clocking mechanism."*

*Building a verb list*

A list of recommended verbs is a helpful tool. Listen to the verbs the people use and note them. Classify them under a general term, as Table 7–1. This will become a valuable guide in any kind of writing. The list below is only one example.

**Table 7–1** Verb list

| Works | Creates | Gives | Gets |
|---|---|---|---|
| attaches | designs | delivers | accepts |
| changes | develops | distributes | compiles |
| conducts | starts | issues | gathers |
| destroys | installs | mails | keeps |
| enters | plans | releases | obtains |
| files | schedules | routes | picks-up |
| inserts | | sends | pulls |
| makes | | ships | recalls |
| marks | | submits | receives |
| moves | | supplies | secures |
| operates | | | takes |
| places | **Controls** | | |
| prepares | charges | | |
| records | checks | | |
| runs | corrects | **Studies** | **Tells** |
| separates | counts | analyzes | advises |
| sorts | edits | compares | assigns |
| stamps | inspects | evaluates | notifies |
| totals | ensures | forecasts | orders |
| uses | logs | identifies | recommends |
| writes | measures | reads | |
| | weighs | surveys | |

## Adjectives

Adjectives describe things. Instead of saying *"The house...,"* we can add a word to describe the house, such as: *"The old house..."* Adjectives are extremely valuable, but they can also turn into clutter very quickly.

Twain was very emphatic on adjectives. He said:

*"When you catch an adjective, kill it. No, I don't mean utterly, but kill most of them—then the rest will be valuable. They weaken when they are close together. They give strength when they are wide apart."*

Once you get passed the comic opening line of this paragraph, there's some awfully good advice about adjectives. Use them carefully.

### Adverbs

Like adjectives, adverbs are descriptive words. They describe how things are done.

*"Turn knob slowly…"*

*"Bring together quickly…"*

The same advice of moderation serves for adverbs also. Use them too frequently and they can become clutter.

There is another thing to be wary of with adverbs. They can become qualifiers and can open doors you do not want opened. You will always have people asking you "How quickly is *quickly*?" And when you use qualifiers like "usually" or "normally," you can be asked about the unusual or abnormal situation.

### Some helpful hints

- Be careful of "…of…" phrases.

  *"The table lists the points of test…"*

  or

  *"The table lists the test points…"*

- Superfluous words

  *"Turn the knob in a clockwise direction…"*

  or

  *"Turn the knob clockwise…"*

  and

  *"At that point in time…"*

  or

  *"Then…"*

- Misplaced modifiers

  *"One morning I shot an elephant in my pajamas. How he got in there, I'll never know."*

- Redundancies

  *"10 am in the morning..."*

  *"Little round circles..."*

Words are the basic building blocks we use for our communication, verbal or written. I suppose the important thing to emphasize is to become sensitive to words. We need to develop a new appreciation for the simple word, need to appreciate a word's nuance and meaning.

## Sentences

We put words together to form sentences. In its simplest form, the sentence contains an actor and an action—someone or something does something. One of the simplest and most effective sentences comes from the New Testament. It is two words.

*"Jesus wept."*

These two words make up a complete sentence: an actor and an action. If you don't have these two items, you don't have a complete sentence.

Simple sentences have only one clause—one actor and one action—like the example above. Sometimes another piece that tells what or who is added.

*"The clerk enters the work order number."*

This is still a simple sentence. One actor—"*The clerk...*"—and one action—"*...enters...*". The added information is what is entered: "*...the work order number.*" You could even add another element—where the work order number is entered, "*...in the log book.*"—and still have a simple sentence.

If you join two simple sentences together with a conjunction—and, but, or—you can build a compound sentence.

> *"The clerk enters the work order in the log book and at the end of each day the clerk tabulates the number of entries."*

This sentence is made up of two complete sentences. The clerk is the actor in both, but the actions are separate.

There are also complex sentences and compound-complex sentences, but they are not often of use in the type of writing we are doing.

Sometimes, we run a risk of confusion when we use compound sentences.

The best advice is to use simple sentences.

> *"The clerk completes the entry in the log book. At the end of the day, the clerk tabulates the entries. The clerk takes the log book to the manager at the end of the day."*

This is much clearer. There are fewer chances of confusion.

### Keep sentences specific and concrete

> *"When the action of an object or an operation has been deemed satisfactory by those who operate it or who use the finished product or service, it is not imperative, indeed, even required, that any maintenance operations be taken to correct any real or imagined faults in the process or object."*

How easy, it seems, for us to forget our original intention was to communicate.

## Paragraphs

Sentences are collected into paragraphs.

The paragraph should be limited to one idea or topic. Everything in the paragraph should contribute to that central idea or topic.

There is a dictum: "The only good paragraph is a short paragraph." It isn't a bad rule of thumb, but it might not serve in all circumstances and situations.

A paragraph should be as long or as short as it needs to be.

In the traditional sense, the first sentence of the paragraph should tell what the paragraph is about. It is called the "topic sentence." The last sentence of the paragraph may serve both as a conclusion and a bridge to the next paragraph.

## Types of Writing Required

Now that we've looked at some fundamentals of writing, let's look at all the different places where the fundamentals may be applied.

### Notes

We talked about taking notes in the section on planning the audit. The auditor should leave space on his or her audit plan for notes, but be cautious against taking too many notes. When the auditor is taking notes he or she is not listening, and listening is where the auditor gets the information.

Although the auditor's notes may become part of the record of the audit, the auditor doesn't have to pay attention to good writing when taking notes. The notes primarily are for the auditor, and no one has to read them but the auditor. To keep the time taking notes to a minimum, auditors should develop a shorthand for themselves.

### Nonconformance reports

Whenever the auditor finds something that is not in compliance, he or she must record it. Usually, nonconformances are recorded on a form. The form might be called a "Discrepancy Report," or "Non Conformity Report (NCR)" or a "Corrective Action Request (CAR)." It doesn't matter what the form is called, it has the same purpose, and, generally, they look alike also. I have included a generic form in Figure 7–1, but whatever the auditor runs across generally resembles this form.

### Description and discussion

*Report #*
This is a control number, and it differs from system to system. Usually, each NCR has its own number. This number is a convenience in referring to the report, and it is a handy recordkeeping practice.

*Department*
This is where the audit was conducted, where the noncompliance was found; i.e., "Production," "Purchasing," etc.

*Date*
This is the date of the audit.

*Details*
This section is where the auditor writes the details of the noncompliance. This is the auditor's area. How this is completed is covered later in this section.

*Corrective Action*
This is where the audit subject, usually management personnel responsible for the area, write the corrective action taken or the corrective action planned to address the noncompliance.

*Submitted/Acknowledged*
These are blocks for signatures. The auditor's signature goes in the "submitted by" box, and the audit subject—whoever received the report—goes in the "acknowledged by" box. The reason the audit subject is asked to sign is proof that the results of the audit have been brought to their attention.

<table>
<tr><td colspan="2" align="center">Jerry-Rigg Manufacturing<br>Nonconformance Report</td></tr>
<tr><td>Department: ____________</td><td>Report #: ____________<br>Date: ____________</td></tr>
<tr><td colspan="2" align="center">Details:</td></tr>
<tr><td colspan="2" align="center">Corrective Action:</td></tr>
<tr><td>Submitted: ____________</td><td>Acknowledged: ____________</td></tr>
<tr><td colspan="2"> NCR Closed: Actions:</td></tr>
<tr><td>By: ____________</td><td>Date: ____________</td></tr>
</table>

**Figure 7–1** Nonconformance report

*NCR Closed*
This is the area used when follow-up actions have concluded that corrective action has been taken and that it has been effective.

## Writing the details of the noncompliance

Writing the details of the noncompliance is difficult. It is where the auditor focuses the most attention. They appear very simple when they are first read, but there is an art to writing them. The auditor must remember that someone else is going to have to read and understand the details of the noncompliance, is going to be asked to sign the form, and must take corrective actions after the auditor has left.

The details may be written up in many different fashions, depending upon the individual auditor's background, experiences and personal style; however, all details must contain three elements and may contain a fourth element. The three necessary elements all details of non-compliance must have are:

- *Where* the noncompliance is;
- *What* the noncompliance is; and
- *Why* this is a problem, which may include an *explanation* for clarity.

Let's see how it works in the following simple example.

In an engineering department, the auditor observed that drawing #415 was not signed in the signature block that shows review and approval. ISO 9001/2, paragraph 4.5.2 requires that "...all documents be reviewed and approved ...prior to issue..."

There is a noncompliance here. A drawing has been found that does not comply with the ISO 9000 standard. The required three elements of writing this noncompliance could go like this:

- *Where* is the noncompliance? The write up should identify precisely where the noncompliance is. If the form allows the auditor to identify the department or area, then that may not be repeated. The write up may start like this:

  *"Engineering drawing #415..."*

  When that is read, is there any doubt exactly where the noncompliance is? There shouldn't be. It is on engineering drawing #415.

- *What* is the noncompliance?

  *"...has no evidence of review and approval."*

  Notice the language here is not accusatory, incriminating, or personal. It is a simple statement of fact. The fact is there is no evidence that this page of the drawing was ever reviewed and approved. The auditor is not saying the document wasn't reviewed and approved; the auditor is only saying that there is no evidence of this review and approval. The auditor is not finding fault or trying to blame anyone for this noncompliance. It is a simple statement of fact.

  Now, if the auditor stopped right here, the audit subject would have every right to look at the auditor and say, "So what?" The auditor needs one thing more.

- *Why* is this a problem?

  *"This does not comply with ISO 9001, paragraph 4.5.1."*

  There should be no doubt in anyone's mind why this is a problem. This is a problem because the organization is not doing what the standard requires. Their practice is not in compliance with the requirements of the standard. This nonconformance could be written against the standard or their own procedure or both. It is the definition of why this is a problem, why it must be addressed and corrected.

- *An explanation.*
  The auditor may want to add an explanation which explains the details of the nonconformance. It might go like this:

  *"...which says: 'All documents shall be reviewed and approved...prior to issue...'"*

  The explanation clarifies the "why" of the problem. For an explanation, the auditor may quote—exactly—what the standard or reference says. If the auditor believes the nonconformance is clear without an explanation, they may omit it, but when in doubt, *explain.*

Together the elements would look like this:

*"Engineering drawing #415 has no evidence of review and approval. This does not comply with ISO 9001, paragraph 4.5.2, which states: 'Documents shall be reviewed and approved...prior to issue...' "*

No audit subject should have any problem reading, understanding and signing a noncompliance written this clearly and completely. And should be able to take action to correct the problem. There are no questions left to ask. We know where, what, and why, and that's all we really need.

Let's look at another example:

In a clean room where plastic components that are used in medical devices are assembled, it is required by company procedure, SOP #9, that all personnel wear complete clean room garb while in the room. The auditor notices that two employees are not wearing plastic booties over their shoes.

The nonconformance may be written as:

*Two employees were observed not wearing plastic shoe covers while working in the clean room. This is not in compliance with SOP #9, which requires that complete clean room garb be worn in the clean room.*

Now, you will notice that in neither of these examples are people named. The auditor never wants to ascribe noncompliances to individuals. Remember, the auditor is not doing a personnel appraisal. The auditor is not criticizing or blaming. The auditor is looking for compliance and noncompliance.

### Majors and minors

Third-party auditors often use a system of "major" and "minor" noncompliances. There is no reason to classify noncompliances with any other type of auditing. The third-party auditors do it to make a determination if the company is to be recommended for registration or not. Second-party auditors may use a similar system to determine the likelihood of doing business with a company. Internal auditors should never use such a system.

- Minor. A minor noncompliance is a single lapse in a requirement. For example, there is a document control procedure in place and it seems to be fully implemented, but the auditor finds an obsolete document being used in a particular area. This is an example of a minor noncompliance; it is a single lapse.
- Major. Major noncompliances are a complete breakdown in either the system or the implementation. A required procedure doesn't exist, or the procedure exists but no one is following it. This a complete breakdown in the system.

There is another method of determining a major noncompliance and it is an accumulation of related minor noncompliances. If all the auditors on a team are finding the same sort of minor document control noncompliances, the team leader may take that as evidence of a complete breakdown in the system. How many minors does it take to make a major? I don't know. This is subjective. It is up to the team leader.

Classifying noncompliances isn't an easy business. Over my years of teaching lead assessor courses, it has always been a stumbling block for many of the delegates. Although the definition sounds pretty cut and dried, applying it is not all that easy and it really isn't required.

Third-party auditors use this system to determine recommendations. If the audited organization has a major noncompliance it will not be recommended for registration and another audit will be required. An organization may be recommended for registration with minor noncompliances, when they have been corrected and evidence has been submitted to the registrar.

A second-party auditor may want to use a system like this to assist the client organization in deciding whether or not to accept the audited organization as a supplier. It isn't necessary, but it might be helpful.

Internal auditors should work to the rule that all noncompliances—no matter how severe or inconsequential they might think them—require corrective action. An internal auditor program manager once told me he used the major and minor classification of noncompliance to "...help my managers set priorities." First of all, it isn't the auditor's job to help managers set priorities and, secondly, if a manager needs someone to help him or her set priorities, he or she is overpaid.

My recommendation for internal audit programs is to forget about classifying noncompliances. They are noncompliances and that's that.

## Audit Reports

Audit reports may come in different shapes and sizes. In an internal audit, the audit report may be a simple "audit summary" form. In second- or third-party audits, the audit report is more formal.

## The audit summary

While there may not be any official requirement for an audit report or summary with internal audits, it is very helpful to have one. If the auditor only reports noncompliances, as is required by the ISO 9000 standard, the result is negative. Only the negative things are reported. There is no place in the noncompliance forms to write the positive things, or to make a recommendation or a suggestion. And, when someone needs to review the internal audit program, they must pour through all the reports of noncompliances.

The necessity of the summary was born.

Often these audit summaries are simple, single page affairs. They offer nothing more than a summary of the audit's activities with any added comments, recommendations, and suggestions the auditor may choose to make. They are signed, just as the noncompliance reports are signed, and they become a part of the record of this audit.

An audit summary form may look like Figure 7–2.

### Explanation

This form is pretty self-explanatory. The key points about it are:

- Keep it short and simple—the summary portion should only highlight things found during the audit.
- As before, the responsible person should acknowledge the audit by signing the audit report.
- This form may be used to write positive things about the audit; if only NCRs are completed, there is no chance to write anything positive, but it can be added here.

| **Jerry-Rigg Manufacturing<br>Audit Summary Report** | |
|---|---|
| **Department:** ______________ | **Date:** ______________ |
| **Summary:** | |
| **Submitted:** ______________ | **Acknowledged:** ______________ |

**Figure 7–2** Audit summary

## Audit reports

In larger, more formal audits the audit report is larger and more formal. Often the client company provides the auditor with the format, and the auditor plugs in the specific information about this particular audit. So the format for the report may differ, but the contents are generally as shown in Table 7–2.

**Table 7–2** Contents of an audit report

| Title | Comments |
|---|---|
| Executive Summary | A one-page summary of the audit's findings and recommendations. |
| Administration | Information about the company and the team, such as:<br>Type of audit<br>Audit subject name and address<br>Team members<br>Signature of team leader |
| Introduction | General information about the audit, such as:<br>Audit scope<br>Reference documents used<br>Staff that was visited and other contacts<br>Scope of document review (if applicable)<br>Scope of compliance audit |
| Noncompliance reports | The collection of the individual noncompliance reports by the team members |
| Summary and Recommendations | The team leader's summary of the audit findings and the recommendations |

## Audit records

Records should be kept of audits. What records are kept may vary from organization to organization. At a minimum the records should include:

### The noncompliance reports

Both the open and closed NCRs should be in the file. The new auditor should have access to all noncompliances found during the last audit. During this audit, if it is within his or her scope, the auditor may have an opportunity to follow up and close out some of the open NCRs. Remember, follow up actions determine if the corrective action has been taken (implemented) and if it is effective.

Reviewing recently closed-out NCRs is valuable also. This should not influence auditors, but will provide them with a background of the department or activity.

### The audit report

Whether this is a simple summary or a full-blown report, the auditor should review it for additional information not found on the NCRs.

### The audit plan and the auditor's notes

The auditor's plan from the previous audit should be available. Auditors can talk to each other over the weeks and months through the audit plan. If I stumbled across something that was not in the scope of my audit but is nevertheless interesting, I may make a note of it on my plan, and the next auditor may have the opportunity to follow up on it.

## Summary

The written records of audits are not complex. They are all fairly simple and each has a direct, easy-to-understand purpose. This does not make them necessarily easy for the auditor to do. Auditors must hone their writing skills, just as they have to sharpen their interviewing skills.

- Write clear, simple noncompliance reports that explain where, what, and why.
- Write concise summaries that also use the audit summary report form to provide positive information and, perhaps, other observations that don't belong on NCRs.
- Make a good plan and use the plan to reach out to other auditors.

# INDEX